POLICE BOYS

Marion Isaac McClinton

I0140136

BROADWAY PLAY PUBLISHING INC
New York
www.broadwayplaypub.com
info@broadwayplaypub.com

POLICE BOYS
© Copyright 1995 Marion Isaac McClinton

Cover photo by Martha Swope

First published by B P P I in October 2010 in *Plays From Playwrights Horizons, Volume 2*
This edition: November 2018
I S B N: 978-0-88145-728-5

Book design: Marie Donovan
Page make-up: Adobe InDesign
Typeface: Palatino

POLICE BOYS was first produced at Playwrights Horizons as part of the New Theater Wing, on 22 June 1994. The cast and creative contributors were:

COMANCHE .... Isaiah Washington
ROYAL BOY .... Akili Prince
CROSS .... Russell Andrews
BOWIE .... Leland Gantt
JABALI .... Chuck Cooper
BABE RUTH .... Oni Faida Lampley
FELLOWS/LADY IN WHITE .... Eliza Ventura
THE SIGNIFYING MONKEY .... Larry Gilliard, Jr

Director .... Donald Douglass
Sound design .... Don DiNicola
Fight direction .... David Leong
Casting .... Janet Foster
Production manager .... Jack O'Connor
Production stage manager .... Jana Llynn

POLICE BOYS was subsequently produced at Playwrights Horizons on the Mainstage, with the first performance on 14 May 1995. The cast and creative contributors were:

COMANCHE .... Richard Brooks
ROYAL .... Akili Prince
CROSS .... Russell Andrews
BOWIE .... Leland Gantt
JABALI .... Chuck Cooper
BABE RUTH .... Nancy Giles
FELLOWS/LADY IN WHITE .... Judith Hawking
THE SIGNIFYING MONKEY .... Larry Gilliard, Jr

Director .... Donald Douglass
Scenic design .... Riccardo Hernandez
Costume design .... Judy Dearing
Lighting design .... Jan Kroeze
Incidental music & sound design .... Don DiNicola
Fight direction .... David Leong
Casting .... Janet Foster
Production manager .... Jack O'Connor
Production stage manager .... Andrea J Testani

CHARACTERS & SETTING

The Lady In White
Sergent Ruth "Babe Ruth" Milano
The Signifying Monkey
Benjamin Santiago Bowie
Meredith Fellows
Captain Jabali Abdul LaRouche
Christopher "Comanche" Chileogus Cummings
The Royal Boy
Cross "Superboy" Beauchamp

A future you can touch with your hand.

The play takes place in the community affairs room, the captain's office, and the holding cell of a police station.

ACT ONE

THE SIGNIFYING MONKEY:
Deep down in the jungle
So they say
There's a signifying monkey
Coming down the way
There wasn't no mess in the jungle
for quite a bit
Till up jumped the monkey saying
"Guess I'll raise some shit!"
(Beat)
Behani ghani, motherfuckers! I was in the general
vicinity, so I thought I would make a stop by, and
mess wit y'all's head for a minute. Can you dig it?
Have you dug it? Was you there Mister Charlie
when they lynched my savior on the cross? Yes? No?
Don't know—can't tell—don't give a rat's ass in hell?
Shit...I know, I know. You can't win for losing, ain't
got nothing but buzzard luck, can't kill nothing and
won't nothing die. The world got you hanging by a
thread, and ain't throwing you nothing but scissors,
you a blind man marching to a different drummer
right through a glass window (can't see no panes, but
you sure as shit gonna feel it!), because like fuck that
Gertrude Stein bitch, money, there is a there there. And
it's a mother and a half, brother. Just ask all them boys
with all of them gats in their hands, The ones playing
Russian roulette twenty-four-seven, five bullets loaded

with only a single empty chamber. You know what I'm saying? *(Beat)*

Yeah…I know. That shit don't move you to tears… right? What use are the little motherfuckers anyways? Ain't got a thing to do with you, you just passing through your own reality, and ain't picking up no hitch hikers. Ain't that why you signed that contract wit Ammmmmerica? *(Beat)*

Well, that's why I'm here. *(Beat)*

In Nigeria, I am Esu-Elegbara, in Brazil I am the almighty Exu, I'm Echu-Elegua in Cuba, and I am the great at them crossroads gates, Papa Legba, in that voodoo you do so well in Haiti. Baby…I'm a divine motherfucker, and I am wicked and can kick it like Wilson Pickett. I can pimp your soul around the block like a one dollar ho what gives change, and talk enough sweet sounding shit to make a lion take an ass-kicking from an elephant. I'm bad. *(Beat)*

I'm The Signifying Monkey, and if you don't get hip, be wise, and wipe the sleep from out of your eyes… then them boys with them guns in their hands gonna start playing Russian roulette wit six bullets, it's gonna be your turn next. Cuz them boys might not be a part of the contract, and they might not be your creation, but then again, they weren't God's creations either, and the bill is due. Cuz the next motherfucker who gonna have to get up on that old rugged cross to cancel all debts…is gonna be you.

(In the middle of the ritual, CHRISTOPHER "COMANCHE" CHILEOGUS CUMMINGS *reaches for something, and realizes it isn't there. He thinks for a moment about how to complete the ritual. When it comes to him, he closes his eyes and speaks.)*

COMANCHE:
I am the scorn of all my adversaries

A horror to my neighbors
An object of dread to my acquaintances
Those who see me in the street flee from me
I have passed out of mind like one who is dead
I have become a broken vessel
O, I hear the whispering of many
With terror on every side
As they scheme together against me
As they plot to take my life

(Lights and drums begin to swell, surrounding
COMANCHE's *head inside and out. He does a dance*
to complete the ritual. He comes out of it and the THE
SIGNIFYING MONKEY *speaks to him.)*

THE SIGNIFYING MONKEY: What is it you seek?

COMANCHE: I have nothing.

THE SIGNIFYING MONKEY: He who does not search, will
not find.

COMANCHE: What is truth?

THE SIGNIFYING MONKEY: I know the answer to what
you seek, but first you must be of a mind to serve me
as well.

COMANCHE: Command me in all things that you might
hope to want.

THE SIGNIFYING MONKEY: Write your name with your
own blood, and write it upon your soul. I am going to
give you what you wish, but first you must give me
that which you love. Before the clock strikes midnight
twice. And then the truth will become flesh and be
known to you.

COMANCHE: How can I recognize a truth I have never
seen? Can I have a sign?

THE SIGNIFYING MONKEY: I HAVE GIVEN YOU
AUDIENCE AND CEREMONY!!! But I will allow the
Loa to give you a sign. Behold!

(Rising out of the shadows appears THE ROYAL BOY, *who
is dressed in the full regalia of the Police Boys. He pulls a
microphone from out of his pants zipper, and begins to rap.)*

ROYAL BOY:
ALLRIGHT!!! LET'S KICK IT!!!
WE AIN'T APOSTLES OF CHRIST
BUT DISCIPLES OF DOOM
YOU AIN'T WASHED IN THE BLOOD
YOU BEST GIVE UP SOME ROOM

THE BOYZ SHALL BRACE YA
CONTINUE TO AMAZE YA
ALL THOSE STONE COLD SUCKERS
CAN'T RUN IN OUR RACE YA

PUT THEM CRIPPLES IN THEIR PLACE
BUST SOME BOOTY IN THEIR FACE
EXPLODE THEIR GOD DAMNED SOUL
INTO FUCKING OUTER SPACE

WE AIN'T NO TOYS
GOT TOO MUCH POISE
YOU WANNA BEAT DOWN SOME NOISE
YOU GONNA BRING ON THE BOYZ

DON'T FUCK WITH THE BOYZ
POLICE BOYS!!!
DON'T DON'T DONTDONTDONTDONTDONT
  DONTDONTDONT
DO NOT FUCK WIT THE BOYZ!!!
YO!!!

WE DON'T STUTTER
CAN'T STAMMER IN MIND
WE BASE LAME MOTHERFUCKERS
DIS TITTY BABY CRIMES

YOUR HEART GOES PITTER PATTER
AS OUR AUTOMATICS SCATTER
WE WHIP YOUR HEAD LIKE BATTER
FOR YOU KNOW WHAT'S THE MATTER

WE PROPHETS OF MURDER
AIN'T YOU HEARD OF
ALL THE BAD BURNERS AND BLOOD CURDLERS

WE PASS OUT TRAGEDY
YOU KNOW WE HAD TO BE
SMASHING MOTHERFUCKERS
WEAK COCKSUCKERS

FROM MIAMI'S HEAT
TO SEATTLE'S RAIN
FROM THE EAST TO THE WEST
WHO DON'T KNOW OUR NAME

OUR WISDOM'S TIGHT
OUR CREW IS PROUD
WE ONLY TURN OUR CHEEK
TO THE DEVIL'S CROWD

CUZ AIN'T NOTHING DEF
FROM OUR TIME OF BIRTH
ALL THE MEEK GET
IS SIX FEET OF EARTH

CUZ JEHOVAH BLEEDS A FOOL
ON THE EDGE OF A KNIFE
LEAVING NO KIND OF WITNESS
BUT DEATH OVER LIFE

SO PARTY FREAKY HARDY
AIN'T NO RIGHT NOR WRONG
MY BIBLE IS A BULLET
AK-47 PSALM

THIS AIN'T RUN DMZ
BUT A WARRIOR CHANT
I'LL SNATCH YOUR HEART THROUGH YOUR

SOUL
IN THE PALM OF MY HAND

DON'T FUCK WIT THE BOYZ!!!
POLICE BOYS!!!
DON'T DON'T DONTDONTDONTDONTDONT
  DONTDONT
DON'T MESS WITH THE BOYZ!!!
WORD UP, AND PEACE OUT, MOTHERFUCKERS!!!

(A LADY IN WHITE *appears in a white jogging suit. She sees* ROYAL BOY *and tries to get away. He pulls a butterfly blade, twirls it open, and places it to her throat. She freezes instantly.)*

ROYAL BOY: Where do you think you going, bitch?

(They both freeze as lights cross fade back to COMANCHE *as the drums return.* COMANCHE *does a chant, during which* CAPTAIN JABALI ABDUL LAROUCHE *enters the Community Affairs room, noticing* COMANCHE *warily.)*

COMANCHE: …and the universal soul begat the human who begat the racial who begat the sexual begat the national begat the ancestral begat the astral begat the historical begat the personal soul to the life of that which binds us to the blood of ourselves, each other, and the things to come…. Amen.

JABALI: May I help you?

COMANCHE: Captain.

JABALI: Comanche?

COMANCHE: Yes sir.

JABALI: Nice to have you back, Sergeant.

COMANCHE: Thank you, sir.

JABALI: I didn't quite recognize you at first.

COMANCHE: Yes sir.

JABALI: I mean with the bald head and everything else…

COMANCHE: Of course you didn't sir.

JABALI: So you see how that might happen. Me not recognizing a police officer, in my station house, that looks like something out of *Tales from the Crypt.* You can see that?

COMANCHE: Warriors of West African Islamic faith shave their heads as a symbol of piety, Captain.

JABALI: I'm quite aware of that, Comanche.

COMANCHE: They also customarily shave their scalps after the death of a blood relative, sir.

JABALI: Has a blood relative of yours died recently that you know of?

COMANCHE: I have no blood relatives I can remember, Captain.

JABALI: I'm sorry, Comanche. I didn't mean for it to come out that way.

COMANCHE: I was doing it for A J, Captain. *(Beat)* Do you know why A J killed himself, sir?

JABALI: You sure you were doing this for A J…or for yourself?

COMANCHE: I…I guess I'm not exactly sure, sir. Do you know why A J did it, Captain?

JABALI: Did what?

COMANCHE: Kill himself.

JABALI: This ritual you were doing, how was it supposed to work?

COMANCHE: You mix skull shavings with some other things in this bowl to ward off… I'm not exactly sure what I was warding off, but I'm sure it was something that had better be warded. I was also supposed to beat

off the evil energy and the spirits of the dead with a
bullwhip but I forgot the whip at home so I couldn't
use the proper recitation, so I ad-libbed Psalm 31,
verses 11 through 13 instead, sir.

JABALI: And you expected that to work, Sergeant?

COMANCHE: In theory sir, I guess. I don't know, sir. I
mean if I had the whip I think...

JABALI: This is a police station, Sergeant. Don't do what
you don't know how to do here.

COMANCHE: Yes sir.

JABALI: Put on your uniform shirt, dump out your skull
shavings, and leave the whip home tomorrow as well.

COMANCHE: Yes sir.

JABALI: Benjamin Bowie has been reassigned to the
Untouchables. I could have you back on the condition
that you were under Bowie's observation for a
probationary period. That's an order. Can you handle
that?

COMANCHE: Yes sir. Benjamin Bowie and the Big
Bed are old friends. They don't mean anything to me
anymore, Captain. I finally finished my studies, and
passed the bar. I'm a lawyer now.

JABALI: I know. That's the only reason they are
allowing you back.

COMANCHE: That's a nice way of putting it.

JABALI: Comanche. You were bar none the best police
officer I have ever seen. I don't doubt you will be all of
that again. But that voodoo you were playing with, it
wasn't Yoruba, it was Haitian. My father was Haitian.
I know two or three things about walking the night.
Some gods are best prayed to from a distance. Some
get pretty rough up close. Especially if you are calling
down a truth whose name you do not know.

COMANCHE: I'll be fine, Captain. The jungle is afraid of the night, but I'm not afraid of either anymore. I even requested duty without a weapon.

JABALI: That's not normal for a cop, Comanche. But I am running short on bodies, and you know the drill. So, welcome back, Sergeant. Clean yourself up, Comanche. You're on duty as of now.

COMANCHE: Thank you, Captain. Oh, and sir?

JABALI: Yes?

COMANCHE: You got one coming.

JABALI: One what?

COMANCHE: You got one coming who will burn your fingers to the bone.

(Just at that moment SERGEANT RUTH "BABE RUTH" MILANO, *and* OFFICER CROSS "SUPERBOY" BEAUCHAMP *bring in* ROYAL BOY, *who is kicking and screaming.)*

ROYAL BOY: RAISE UP OFF ME, MOTHERFUCKER!!

*(*CROSS *and* BABE RUTH *pull* ROYAL BOY *down into a chair.)*

ROYAL BOY: GET YOUR CLAWS OFF ME, BITCH!!!

BABE RUTH: Take your hat off inside of the building.

CROSS: Where were you raised, in a sewer, rat?

ROYAL BOY: Kiss my ass, punk!

CROSS: TAKE THAT HAT OFF LIKE SHE SAID!!!

JABALI: Stay on task, people.

ROYAL BOY: I don't take this hat off in your little old gray haired momma's holy rolling, tongue speaking, motherfucking church. Fuck you, bitch!

*(*CROSS *snatches the hat off of* ROYAL BOY.)*

ROYAL BOY: Just can't keep your hands off me, huh, baby?

(CROSS *grabs* ROYAL BOY *and is about to strike him.*)

JABALI: That's enough.

ROYAL BOY: Shit. You too easy for the kid, punk! I'll have you on my dick in another minute.

CROSS: I'LL BE ON YOUR ASS IN A MINUTE!!!

JABALI: Five dollars for the language, Superboy.

CROSS: CAPTAIN, NOT NOW, NOT IN FRONT OF...

JABALI: Should I make it ten?

CROSS: God dammit, Captain!

JABALI: Now it's ten.

(CROSS *hands over the money.* ROYAL BOY *breaks out laughing.*)

ROYAL BOY: Taking little junior's lunch money away for, like, saying naughty words and shit. Damn!

JABALI: My station house. My house rules.

ROYAL BOY: What are you gonna do to me, wash my mouth out with soap?

JABALI: You can talk all you want.

(*The phone rings in* JABALI'*s office area.*)

JABALI: Comanche! Take over here.

COMANCHE: Yes, Captain. So... You have a name?

ROYAL BOY: I am the Grandmaster Blaster, Big Monster Masher, Secretary of Offense and the Minister of Pain. I am His Almighty Royal Badness, the one, the only, motherfucking, bulldogging Royal Boy in the house.

COMANCHE: What's your name?

BABE RUTH: The one your momma gave you.

CROSS: Cause Lord knows you probably ain't never seen a daddy.

BABE RUTH: Maybe you were just hatched, and left under the nest.

ROYAL BOY: Kiss my ass bitch!

BABE RUTH: Oh, that hurt. Do you have a Christian name?

ROYAL BOY: Shit, baby, you know me! I'm the nigger with the trigger that'll make your stomach grow bigger.

BABE RUTH: This must be one of the educated ones.

COMANCHE: Come again?

(Pause)

ROYAL BOY: William.

COMANCHE: You have any other aliases?

ROYAL BOY: What would I need that shit for, my brother?

CROSS: Cause you a high-rolling, jack-balling baby wannabe, an Original Gangster.

ROYAL BOY: I don't know about no O G T.

BABE RUTH: You just an innocent manchild lost in the promised land?

ROYAL BOY: You ain't never been righter.

COMANCHE: So I don't get it. Why are you here?

ROYAL BOY: You the motherfucking police. You tell me.

COMANCHE: You came here of your own free will?

BABE RUTH: He was fighting and biting and kicking the whole way here.

ROYAL BOY: That's cause you all was running a Rodney King on me, and police brutality-izing me, bitch.

COMANCHE: You were just picked up for no apparent reason?

ROYAL BOY: Man, I was stopped.

COMANCHE: Stopped for what?

ROYAL BOY: Investigation purposes, some such bullshit, I don't know, man. Ask them motherfuckers and shit.

COMANCHE: For just what purpose might we be investigating you for, your Royal Badness?

ROYAL BOY: I ain't got a clue fool.

COMANCHE: You ever been in correctional facilities?

ROYAL BOY: No.

COMANCHE: Ever been to a psychiatrist before?

ROYAL BOY: Hell no. What about you?

CROSS: We ask the questions, punk.

BABE RUTH: You ever been in any kind of trouble with the law?

CROSS: You ever been in a foster home?

ROYAL BOY: No, and no.

BABE RUTH: You got any kind of weapons at home in your playpen?

CROSS: Twenty-twos.

BABE RUTH: Nine millikillers.

CROSS: AK-47s.

BABE RUTH: Missile launchers, or small portable thermonuclear warheads.

ROYAL BOY: No, no, no, no, and let me think for a minute…no.

CROSS: Shoot, even babies nursing off they mama's titties pack a thirty eight in your neighborhood.

ROYAL BOY: I just say "no" to guns, you simple ass punk.

BABE RUTH: Is that a fact?

CROSS: He's got me convinced.

BABE RUTH: You're a real down-for-his-neighborhood kind of guy?

CROSS: Ain't you Royal Punk!

ROYAL BOY: I ain't no punk, man. Fuck with me, and we'll dance a wild motherfucking fandango until the end of the world, you know what I'm saying?

COMANCHE: Then I don't get it, what are you doing here?

ROYAL BOY: Now you understanding my dilemma, brother, because the shit has got me puzzled, too. See, I think your crew is trying to drag a game all over me, trying to gaffle me like I'm the punk of the week, but I didn't go for it. I told them to sugar smack my ass, I ain't no buster slipping on the golden rope like some buzzed out cluckhead. Told them to stack their weak ass shit, and pack it up until Christmas, that they had lost their motherfucking minds. They almost got assed out, man, for not showing a true original black man the like proper respect. I just played along to see what they had on they little, itty-bitty, Mickey Mouse minds.

COMANCHE: You're just an innocent bystander to the harsh realities of life?

ROYAL BOY: Look, brother, you seem to be the intelligent motherfucking nigger in the house. I ain't nothing but a little kid. I'm fourteen going on thirteen, you know what I'm saying? My case is closed before it ever got opened. I ain't done shit, money. I ain't a peewee, a baby child gangster, and don't wanna be nothing but loved. So if y'all ain't got nothing with like the substance of the Pyramids to say to me, then I'm gonna be splitting and spreading, and you can catch my act in heaven, cause I'm gonna Audi 5000 like a motherfucker man. I got homework to do.

JABALI: What about this little work of art here?

(Pause)

ROYAL BOY: Excuse me, sir?

JABALI: Look familiar?

CROSS: Aw, look. The punk done found some manners.

BABE RUTH: Warms my heart.

JABALI: You know this knife?

ROYAL BOY: It's a Filipino butterfly. More antique than weapon. Knives are for people with a death wish these days.

JABALI: I don't want an advertisement. Yours or not?

(JABALI with a sudden quickness slams the knife down on the table, smashing it. Little pieces of crack cocaine are revealed. ROYAL BOY winces as if he physically feels the impact of the smashing of the knife.)

JABALI: Recognize it now?

ROYAL BOY: Never seen it in my life.

JABALI: I recognize something. Imagine my surprise.

CROSS: Whose idea to lay the rock in the handle, punk?

BABE RUTH: Genius work.

JABALI: Yeah, well, not anymore. You found this around where you lifted His Royal Badness, right?

CROSS: Mm-hmmm.

JABALI: Makes you kind of wonder, Your Royal Badness.

BABE RUTH: Rocks on the inside.

JABALI: Whose fingerprints on the out?

CROSS: It don't look good.

COMANCHE: You should seriously consider talking to a lawyer before you say another word. You want a public defender? Wanna make that call?

ROYAL BOY: You mean public pretender. I don't know nothing about nothing about that knife.

JABALI: That's a shame. God helps those who help themselves.

ROYAL BOY: You didn't have to fuck up the knife.

JABALI: Couldn't be helped. You know what I'm saying? Not much you could've done about it.

ROYAL BOY: Fuck you!

JABALI: Yeah, I know. Is he Miranda-ed?

BABE RUTH: I read him, sir.

COMANCHE: You want me to further inform him of his rights as a minor under the law, Captain?

ROYAL BOY: Who is the smooth talking, bald-headed, scar-faced sonuvabitch!

COMANCHE: I am Sergeant Cummings. I'm also a lawyer. Specially assigned to this unit to make sure your constitutional rights protected by law are not violated.

ROYAL BOY: What?

COMANCHE: I make sure you receive due process.

BABE RUTH: Whether you due it, or not.

ROYAL BOY: Man, fuck that. All you saying is you ain't even legal aid. What you pretending to be, man?

COMANCHE: Nothing.

ROYAL BOY: You sure about that?

JABALI: Good help is hard to find.

ROYAL BOY: I'm hip. That's what the Big Bed is saying all the time.

JABALI: You don't say?

COMANCHE: That's straight. That's the Bed all the way.

ROYAL BOY: Y'all too slick. Be putting all them telepathetic suggestions inside of my personalized thoughts, and shit.

BABE RUTH: Is that what happened?

ROYAL BOY: Yeah, something like that.

COMANCHE: Should I continue questioning, Captain?

JABALI: We're not charging him with anything, are we?

COMANCHE: Not right now.

JABALI: So, you here as a friendly, who we mistook for the true owner of that Class-A-felony knife?

ROYAL BOY: I'm so friendly your mamma and daddy will want to adopt me, I'm so friendly.

JABALI: My cup runneth over at the thought.

ROYAL BOY: Anything for the family, my man. Anything for the family.

(Silence)

JABALI: Why don't we have us a little friendly chat in my office. Between brothers.

ROYAL BOY: It's your world, brother. I'm just trying to live in it.

JABALI: I won't need you, Comanche. I don't think we'll need a chaperone. You don't mind do you, your Royal Badness?

ROYAL BOY: Not at all, bleed. Uh, Perry Mason motherfucker, why don't you chase an ambulance, or something? Baby girl, you wanna get me and my cuz here some doughnuts and shit?

(JABALI grabs ROYAL BOY by the scruff of his neck, carrying him into his office.)

ROYAL BOY: Can't you motherfuckers take a joke? It was a joke?

JABALI: This ain't a comedy club, kid. This is a police station.

CROSS: COMANCHE!!!

COMANCHE: How you making it, you big fat gumbo eating sonovabitch?

CROSS: What you mean, fat? This is all hard now.

BABE RUTH: Especially between the ears.

CROSS: I ain't even thinking about your confused ass today. Gots my main nigger back. The Untouchables are back. The Comanche has returned. *(He starts to sing the old Robert Stack* Untouchables *theme.)* Come on, brother, don't leave me out there like that.

*(*COMANCHE *sings it with him. They sing a bit, then wrestle/hug.)*

BABE RUTH: Great. As if the testosterone levels around here weren't bad enough already.

COMANCHE: Hello, Babe Ruth.

BABE RUTH: Now we got your crazy butt around here, too.

COMANCHE: Always, Babe Ruth.

BABE RUTH: How long have you been gone?

COMANCHE: Three hundred and sixty-six days too long.

BABE RUTH: Time flies when you're having fun.

COMANCHE: It's so good to see you.

*(*COMANCHE *kisses* BABE RUTH *on the cheek, then tries to sneak a kiss on the lips. She flips him on his back, and straddles him.)*

COMANCHE: Nice to see things haven't changed all that much.

BABE RUTH: Things always change, Comanche.

CROSS: Like A J.

BABE RUTH: Give it a rest, Cross.

COMANCHE: Do you know how?

CROSS: Oh, we know how, all right.

BABE RUTH: I said squash it.

CROSS: Is that an order, Acting Watch Commander?

BABE RUTH: Advice.

COMANCHE: Acting Watch Commander?

CROSS: The Untouchables are a gender equity equal opportunity employer now.

BABE RUTH: I think we know which between the two of us have our position because of merit.

COMANCHE: When did this happen?

CROSS: Right after A J blew his brains out.

BABE RUTH: Shut up, Cross. It's no longer advice.

COMANCHE: No wonder the Captain looks like a walking time bomb. He and A J go way back. But something else is bothering him. I can't quite put my finger on it. *(Silence)* I say something wrong?

BABE RUTH: You wanted to talk so much, Cross. Why don't you say something now.

CROSS: Not now. Later.

COMANCHE: What's up, brother blood?

BABE RUTH: What's a matter? Fraidy cat got your tongue?

CROSS: I SAID LATER!!!

COMANCHE: It's okay. It ain't that deep, y'all.

CROSS: You wanna know something that has me downright confused, Babe?

BABE RUTH: Watch Commander to you, Officer Beauchamp.

CROSS: That's just acting, but I don't want to lose my train of thought.

BABE RUTH: Then you shouldn't wake up. You having a thought of any kind is just a dream.

CROSS: How can you be a Republican delegate, and a card-carrying union lesbian? Isn't that a what-do-you-call-it? A contradiction of terms?

COMANCHE: WILL YOU SHUT THE HELL UP!!! YOU DON'T WANT TO TALK, SHUT UP!!!

BABE RUTH: I don't need you to take up on my behalf, Comanche. Keep your help to yourself.

COMANCHE: Don't worry.

BABE RUTH: As for you, Beauchamp. Let me put it to you in terms you can understand. I don't like you. I will never like you. You open your mouth, your ignorance escapes, and I'm tired of you running it on me. I am your superior officer now, and until that changes, I plan on making life hell for you because...I really, really don't like you.

COMANCHE: You wrong, Babe Ruth. Nothing has changed.

BABE RUTH: Things change, Comanche. I have some power in here. That's new. I voted Republican, delegated for them, and everything. That also is new.

COMANCHE: Why? I don't understand that.

BABE RUTH: It's getting out of control, somebody gotta do something.

(MEREDITH FELLOWS *enters the Community Affairs room.*)

FELLOWS: I couldn't agree with you more, Sergeant Milano.

BABE RUTH: Then maybe I should recheck my position.

FELLOWS: Is that the kid in with him now? Just answer the question Sergeant, I don't have time for verbal sparring tonight.

BABE RUTH: There are so many questions surrounding you, Assistant Attorney Fellows, that it boggles the mind trying to sift out the exact answer you might want to hear.

FELLOWS: In case you haven't noticed, we are supposed to be on the same side.

BABE RUTH: Strange world isn't it? But you have been having your share of strange bedfellows lately, haven't you, Fellows? I noticed it's kind of hard to tell which side of the bed you been getting up on these days.

FELLOWS: Are you finished?

BABE RUTH: I'm just getting warmed up.

COMANCHE: The Captain has the Royal Boy in his office.

FELLOWS: Thank you. We'll talk later, Sergeant Milano, okay?

BABE RUTH: Why? When did I make governor?

(FELLOWS *stares at* BABE RUTH, *then exits to* JABALI's *office.*)

JABALI: Mighty impressive resume you have, Your Royal Badness.

ROYAL BOY: I keep busy. Look, man, I want to just set the record straight.

JABALI: Straight about what?

ROYAL BOY: Nothing outstanding. One or two things. Hardly worth mentioning.

FELLOWS: Go ahead and mention it. How are you doing, Jabali?

JABALI: Fellows.

FELLOWS: Do you mind?

JABALI: Not at all.

FELLOWS: You were saying?

ROYAL BOY: I was talking to the brother.

FELLOWS: Well now you can talk to me as well.

ROYAL BOY: You don't bullshit around, do you, baby?

FELLOWS: That's right. You want to talk to us, or should we put you in contact with a lawyer?

ROYAL BOY: That's all right, baby. Y'all don't frighten me. Besides I don't need a lawyer. I'm clean and got nothing to hide.

FELLOWS: It's your choice.

ROYAL BOY: Shit, baby, you would be my kind of choice. You fine as wine. Don't be looking like no beastly lizard butt motherfucker, you know what I'm saying?

FELLOWS: Really?

ROYAL BOY: You ain't so bad for a blond-haired, blue-eyed snowgirl.

FELLOWS: Fond of blonds, aren't you?

ROYAL BOY: Last motherfucking resort. Long as the bitch is as cute as you.

FELLOWS: Don't mistake me for somebody else. I'm not cute. The taxpayers don't pay my salary to be cute.

ROYAL BOY: Hope they getting their money's worth.

FELLOWS: You can bank on it.

JABALI: So, what did you want to discuss, your Royal Badness? The Middle East? The state of the economy? The lack of God in our daily lives?

ROYAL BOY: See, brother, that's what I'm talking about. Why your posse gotta be snatching little youngsters like me from off of the bricks with all the truly messed up whacked out madness happening in the world today, man?

JABALI: Why do you think that is?

ROYAL BOY: I don't know, brother. Shit don't make no sense to me.

FELLOWS: So why are you here?

ROYAL BOY: I said I don't know. I ain't down here checking out the tourist season.

FELLOWS: No, I bet you aren't. You want a smoke?

ROYAL BOY: Old snowgirl done checked out all the fly gangster movies, ain't she? Got her Bogart-Cagney shit down tight for a skirt.

FELLOWS: Thank you. You don't mind, do you, Jabali?

JABALI: Go ahead.

ROYAL BOY: What kind of smokes you got?

FELLOWS: Marlboros. Hard backs.

ROYAL BOY: Your high class yuppie ass is into those redneck rebel tobacco-chewing cowboy motherfuckers? Hey, bleed, who the hell is this snowgirl? She your own trophy bitch, or something, you know what I'm saying?

FELLOWS: I am Assistant District Attorney Meredith Fellows. I am neither a redneck rebel tobacco chewing motherfucker, a snowgirl, or a trophy bitch. I prosecute little idiots like you, and get them locked away for the best years of their little sex drives. By the time they get out of jail, they can't even remember how to spell sex.

ROYAL BOY: Man, you better tell this hammer something, man. She don't know me, she better ask somebody.

FELLOWS: I know who you are, I know why you are here, and I'm thoroughly not impressed. I'll rearrange your life. I'll be all over your black ass like a twenty-four hour virus.

JABALI: Fellows, I don't think…

FELLOWS: I didn't ask you for your opinion, Jabali. You understand me?

JABALI: I understand you just fine.

FELLOWS: Good. You understand me, Royal Boy?

ROYAL BOY: Whatever you say, baby. You definitely the man in this room.

FELLOWS: Now can I get to my questions without further delay, Jabali?

JABALI: Is that a request?

FELLOWS: What do you think?

ROYAL BOY: Oh, wow, brother…she just fronked you off like she the goddess of motherfucking darkness.

FELLOWS: How's your friend doing?

ROYAL BOY: Why, what friend would that be I wonder?

FELLOWS: The Big Bad Bed.

ROYAL BOY: Don't know him.

FELLOWS: Really?

ROYAL BOY: Never heard of him.

FELLOWS: What about the Doghouse Maniac? What's he doing for fun and relaxation these days?

ROYAL BOY: That acting hook trick Buster McPunk is cruising the rinks and coming up with nothing but a cold.

JABALI: So you do know the Doghouse Maniac?

ROYAL BOY: Aw, trying to make a comeback like he Frank Furillo and shit. Don't know him.

FELLOWS: You don't know him.

ROYAL BOY: No.

FELLOWS: Sure about that?

ROYAL BOY: Yeah.

FELLOWS: I've heard rumors.

ROYAL BOY: Fuck you.

FELLOWS: Thanks for the offer, but I have to decline. You know what I'm talking about.

ROYAL BOY: Fuck you and your rumors.

FELLOWS: You kind of seem stuck on that phrase. Does mention of the Doghouse Maniac bring back warm memories of your time in juvie reform?

ROYAL BOY: Look, get off my dick, all right? I ain't got a motherfucking thing to say to you about nothing, bitch! I ain't done nothing! I don't know your fish-smelling ass from this bowtie-wearing motherfucker from the man in the moon. I don't know why you got my innocent bystanding butt off the bricks. I ain't even been around no kind of alleyways no kind of ways!

FELLOWS: Who said anything about alleyways? You say anything about alleyways, Jabali?

JABALI: I haven't dreamt anything about alleyways.

FELLOWS: Uh oh! Who said anything about alleyways?

ROYAL BOY: I just want to make sure you don't have me confused with somebody else.

JABALI: Who? Michael Jackson? Mike Tyson?
Madonna? Who?

ROYAL BOY: Man, I ain't got to say shit!

FELLOWS: You don't have to, you are virtually
screaming everything we need to know. You got the
circle of knowledge on your left arm. The heart on fire,
the crossed pitchforks in the eyes of the Jolly Roger,
suspenders down on the right side, oh, and look,
methinks I see the six pointed red, black, and green
Star of David. You are in full dress uniform. You are a
Kissin Cuzzin.

ROYAL BOY: It ain't the Star of motherfucking David,
but the badge of African Pride! You don't know half
the shit you think you do, snowgirl!

FELLOWS: But the half I do know will jump all up your
little ass like stink on shit. No matter what line of
bullshit you think can fade its way past me, I know as
sure as I'm gonna pay taxes and die that you either a
baby banger, or a wild-bunching wannabe homeboy,
but you are not a civilian innocent bystander in this
lifetime. You're from the Cut, and I can just bet I can
place you in a certain alleyway if you give me enough
time to get creative.

JABALI: We also have him for possession of an illegal
weapon full of little joe snow.

FELLOWS: See…I don't have to fool around with you. I
can bury you. You got something to make and trade?
Got something to sell, I'm buying, but it ain't a bull
market, and, quite frankly, my interest is already
waning. You got words, talk!

ROYAL BOY: All right. Alright. I don't wanna fuck with
you. I got it. But I gotta whisper it to you. Not him.
Only you.

FELLOWS: Fine with me.

(FELLOWS *goes over to* ROYAL BOY, *puts her ear to his lips, and he spits in her ear.*)

FELLOWS: YOU FILTHY, DISGUSTING...

ROYAL BOY: I ain't gotta say jack to you without a lawyer, or my legally required adult by my side making sure my rights ain't being fucking violated!

FELLOWS: RIGHTS!!! YOU WANT RIGHTS!!!

ROYAL BOY: I HAVE RIGHTS, BITCH!!! KISS MY MOTHERFUCKING ASS!!!

FELLOWS: YOU LITTLE ASSHOLE!!!

ROYAL BOY: FUCK YOU!!! REMEMBER ESTELENE RAYE? YOU FUCKED HER CASE ALL UP, DIDN'T YOU!!! YOU AIN'T SHIT BITCH!!!

(FELLOWS *leaps at* ROYAL BOY *and is intercepted by* JABALI.)

ROYAL BOY: NAW, MAN, LET THE BITCH BE!!! SHE WANNA LEAP, I'LL RECEIVE!!!

JABALI: SHUT UP!!! CALM DOWN, COUNSELOR!!!

FELLOWS: LET ME GO, GODDAMMIT!!!

JABALI: You all right?

FELLOWS: Let...me...go! I want a word with you, Jabali.

JABALI: Comanche!

COMANCHE: Yo!

JABALI: Keep his Royal Badness company.

FELLOWS: JABALI!!!

ROYAL BOY: Mom's calling, Captain.

(JABALI *glares at* ROYAL BOY, *then goes over to talk to* FELLOWS.)

JABALI: What?

FELLOWS: Don't give me that shit!

JABALI: Language, counselor.

FELLOWS: I'm not playing with you, Jabali!

JABALI: A little respect, a little common courtesy is all I'm asking.

FELLOWS: I don't work for you. I don't have to give you anything I don't believe you have earned.

JABALI: Oh, I'm sure I have earned it. In this house, I have definitely earned that and a whole lot more.

FELLOWS: Really? The citizens of this city are terrified of these gangs, especially the Police Boys, and you are not even giving them a false sense of security. I have it from the Governor himself that the state is about to take over municipal government totally. I have full command of your unit now. You answer directly to me. Nobody else.

JABALI: Since when?

FELLOWS: There's been a changing of the guard. The Commissioner, the Police Chief, have both been relieved of their duties. In case you have forgotten, the state, not the city, has funded your little operation. The Governor has told me personally that if you don't deliver the Big Bad Bed to him on a silver platter in twenty-four hours he will cut off your funding and disband your unit permanently.

(Pause)

JABALI: Nobody wants the Bed more than me. I will do my job.

FELLOWS: What about your posse?

JABALI: They will do their jobs.

FELLOWS: I hope they do a better job than they are getting a reputation for doing.

JABALI: Don't worry. No further miscues.

FELLOWS: Wouldn't that look good on eyewitness news for a change. *(She exits.)*

CROSS: I thoroughly dislike that bitch, Captain.

JABALI: She speaks highly of you, too. Five dollars, Superboy.

(CROSS gives him the money.)

JABALI: If anybody shows up for this kid I want to be notified. Public, a parent, or the werewolf of London, I don't care. I want to talk to them before Fellows, is that clear?

BABE RUTH: Yes, Captain.

CROSS: Damn, Babe, what did you ever see in her anyways?

BABE RUTH: I liked her politics. And you can call me Commander Milano.

JABALI: Comanche?

COMANCHE: Yes sir?

JABALI: I'm gonna see what in the hell is happening within the department. I wanted to be here when Bowie arrived...

COMANCHE: Captain, I've had post-trauma sessions...

JABALI: That's not what I'm saying...

COMANCHE: Until I have had Sigmund Freud coming out of my ass (I owe you five dollars), a thirty day long group session, group therapy, nutritional counseling, and a fitness regimen with a stress management plan, until I can write that shit in my sleep backwards...

JABALI: Now it's ten.

COMANCHE: Make it twenty, fifty, a million, it don't matter. I am back, Captain. Reunited and together again. I'm in touch with my Nommo Force and in total communion with my astral self.

JABALI: Comanche…

COMANCHE: I'll be all right with Bowie.

(BENJAMIN SANTIAGO BOWIE *enters the Community Affairs room on* COMANCHE'*s last couple of lines unseen.*)

BOWIE: It's just great seeing you again, too, Comanche. Old friends like us should stay in touch.

ROYAL BOY: Shit, old boy is Humphrey Bogart like a motherfucker.

JABALI: Comanche…take the kid downstairs and run him for priors.

COMANCHE: I thought you had his files.

JABALI: Do what I tell you, Sergeant.

COMANCHE: Yes sir.

JABALI: This is for the both of you. No vendettas inside of my command. All hatchets blunted and buried.

BOWIE: All I ever did was honor the letter of the law.

JABALI: You wouldn't be able to recognize honor if you tripped over it.

BOWIE: I know what the truth is, Captain, just as well as you do. I have been assigned by Psychiatric to observe your men. Be there for…support. Help out in any way I can.

JABALI: I don't like unzipping my pants and finding somebody else's hand in there, Sergeant. Take note.

BOWIE: Noted.

JABALI: With A J and Miller down, I'm short of men who know the bricks. You will obey my orders, or I will have you written up for insubordination. And that will be the least of your worries if you cross me. Understand?

BOWIE: I'm not stupid, Captain. I know my back's exposed.

JABALI: Smart man. Take a seat in my office, and we'll get reacquainted for a minute.

BOWIE: As you wish, *Mon Capitaine*. We gotta catch up with each other, Comanche. As a matter of fact, we'll have to. It's my job. We have so much to talk about, don't you think?

JABALI: Come on, Comanche… Take the kid like I said.

COMANCHE: Yes sir. Here's your ten dollars, Captain.

JABALI: That's okay, Comanche. First day back. You get a freebie.

COMANCHE: That's okay. I pay my debts. I don't like to owe things to anybody.

JABALI: I hate days that start at midnight.

(Lights change as THE SIGNIFYING MONKEY *sneaks up behind* COMANCHE, *and whispers in his ear. Everybody else freezes in time and space.)*

THE SIGNIFYING MONKEY:
Vision well, my little brother.
Cuz Jesus lost His laugh
While fallen angels slipped
Keep hope alive is dying
As the Holy Ghost slept
Sing a song, my brother
In your daddy's pockets
You in the army now
Your case has made the docket
Vision well, my brother, cuz
There ain't no use in trying
Cuz can't a motherfucker stop
This monkey
From signifying.

(Lights and time return to normal. It is now five o'clock in the morning. COMANCHE *snaps out of it, and puts* ROYAL BOY *in the holding cell.)*

ROYAL BOY: Come on, man, give me back my hat, cuz!

COMANCHE: Sorry.

BABE RUTH: Just throw the punk in the cage, Comanche.

ROYAL BOY: I gotta go to the can, man!

BABE RUTH: You should have went while you were out.

ROYAL BOY: I didn't have to go then.

CROSS: You got a drinking cup in there, brother. Go in that.

ROYAL BOY: WHAT?

CROSS: What you squawking at? You gotta go, you gotta go.

BABE RUTH: Or maybe you should practice learning how to keep your fly shut.

ROYAL BOY: Alright. No problems. *(He starts pissing in the cup.)* "I'm singing in the rain, just singing in the rain. What a glorious feeling. I'm…aaaaahhhhhh!… happy again!" Like the man said, gotta go, gotta go.

CROSS: HEY! THIS FOOL IS REALLY PISSING IN THE CUP, MAN!

BABE RUTH: YOU SICK, NASTY, LITTLE DEGENERATE!!!

*(*JABALI *and* BOWIE *exit* JABALI's *office.)*

JABALI: Babe Ruth!

BABE RUTH: Captain?

JABALI: You have something for me?

BABE RUTH: Nobody from Public knows he's here yet, but it's only a matter of time before somebody will get assigned to him. Comanche got a number from him, and I've been checking it, but the person isn't in. I think it's a halfway house.

JABALI: You have an address?

BABE RUTH: I can get one easily enough.

JABALI: Then get it, and check it out. Also check any local tavern, church, what have you. We can do a two step around the public defender for a little while longer, but our hands are tied until we have contact with the L R A.

BABE RUTH: I can also run down the home base address at the halfway house.

JABALI: Good thinking. Anything else?

BABE RUTH: Comanche did that double check on priors, and really came up with nothing but nickel and dime stuff, but the boy does have a taste for violent confrontations. Got bounced out of the school system for it. Attacked a teacher with a knife.

JABALI: Check and see if it's the same knife?

BABE RUTH: I'm having them fax me the material as we speak, Captain. He's also done some interesting time down in juvie reform.

JABALI: I know.

BABE RUTH: So we know where his fear lives. My guess is that he was auditioning for the Police Boys, this stinks of another Wild Bunch attack.

JABALI: It's got all the classic markings.

BABE RUTH: But I hear tell the word on the bricks is that the Big Bad Bed ran this Wild Bunch spree himself.

JABALI: We got witnesses to that?

BABE RUTH: Well, if the victim recovers we have one. Everybody else has developed amnesia as far as a grand jury goes, and is as blind as a bat, too.

JABALI: Check out what people have heard, and see if you can do some new math with it, and make it add up.

BABE RUTH: I got a couple of angles. Anything else before I hit it?

JABALI: With A J gone, that makes you acting watch commander. I'm putting you in for the permanent title, and the promotion that goes along with it.

BABE RUTH: Thanks, Captain.

JABALI: No thanks needed. You've earned it. But because of them games people play downtown, when you and I are gone that means Bowie has the command. That leaves me more uncomfortable than one hundred years of constipation.

BABE RUTH: I get back so fast they won't even notice I'm gone.

JABALI: Keep a tight fist wrapped around things today.

BABE RUTH: My favorite way to play the game, Captain. How are you making it, Captain?

JABALI: I'm fine. Just a lot of things piled on top of one another, but I'll be alright. Don't stay out late.

BABE RUTH: Be back as soon as I can. (*She exits.*)

JABALI: All right, Listen up! I gotta check out ballistics, run by H Q downtown, and swing by the hospital and see how my son is doing.

COMANCHE: What?

JABALI: If the Royal Boy's L R A gets here before I get back, I want either Comanche or Babe Ruth to deal with the situation. I want the L R A to be kept away from you-know-who until I have had a chance to run my questions.

COMANCHE: I understand, sir.

JABALI: Don't break anything in the cage, Superboy.

CROSS: I ain't done nothing!

JABALI: Just see that you don't, or you will have me to deal with, you follow me?

CROSS: Yes sir.

COMANCHE: So Babe Ruth is in charge while you are gone, right, Captain?

JABALI: Completely.

CROSS: SHIT!

(Without waiting for JABALI to ask for it CROSS just reaches into his pocket and takes out the five and hands it to JABALI.)

JABALI: You might as well get a Visa card, Superboy.

CROSS: Yes sir, I think I'll do that.

COMANCHE: Who's in charge until Babe Ruth gets back?

JABALI: Sergeant Bowie.

(CROSS gets out another five and hands it to JABALI.)

CROSS: Motherfucker!

JABALI: All right then. We don't make the world, we just deal with it. *(He exits.)*

COMANCHE: How long has the Captain's son been in the hospital?

CROSS: Not long.

COMANCHE: Is it serious?

BOWIE: A lot of things have been serious lately, haven't they Cross?

COMANCHE: You know about this?

ROYAL BOY: I know what the fuck is wrong with the motherfucker's son.

CROSS: You shut the fuck up!

COMANCHE: Somebody tell me something!

BOWIE: Jabali's son is in the hospital. Intensive care. Touch and go.

COMANCHE: What happened?

BOWIE: Why don't you ask your protégé?

COMANCHE: Superboy? *(Silence)* Well?

ROYAL BOY: Three guesses, motherfucker, and the first two don't count.

CROSS: MAN, I'M WARNING YOU...

ROYAL BOY: You got me scared. I'ze shitting oblong French-perfumed bricks, you got me so petrified.

COMANCHE: You trying to tell me it was the Police Boys?

CROSS: Yeah.

COMANCHE: Man, what in the hell is going on here? You telling me the Police Boys tried to whack the Captain's own son? What's the story?

BOWIE: You been out of touch too long, Comanche. Cross the Superboy has been trying to fill your shoes while you've been gone.

COMANCHE: What's he talking about, man?

BOWIE: I'm interested to hear your rationale behind what happened myself.

CROSS: Fuck you!

BOWIE: Can't really get very much from that.

COMANCHE: Come on, Superboy.

BOWIE: Come on, Superboy.

ROYAL BOY: Come on, Superboy!

CROSS: Punk, I have already done told you…

ROYAL BOY: My momma done told me!

CROSS: Motherfucker!

ROYAL BOY: OOOOPS!!! Methinks you owes me five dollars, Superpunk!

CROSS: YOU WANT ME TO GIVE YOU SOMETHING, SUCKER!!!

COMANCHE: Relax, Cross!

BOWIE: Don't worry, Comanche. He ain't going to do a thing to that boy. Not his style. The boy is too old.

COMANCHE: What are you talking about?

CROSS: Man, fuck the imitation white boy slave-ass niggerhead!

BOWIE: What was that?

ROYAL BOY: Imitation white boy slave-ass niggerhead!

COMANCHE: Man, shut up!

ROYAL BOY: I'd whip his ass behind that slave-ass niggerhead shit, if I was you!

BOWIE: Ain't nothing between Superboy and me but fear and atmosphere.

CROSS: I oughta tie my foot dead-off in your ass, bitch!

BOWIE: What are you waiting for, somebody to hand you some rope?

ROYAL BOY: I don't know, I might be wrong, but I believe he just POOOOWWWW!!!! DISSED YOU BIG TIME!!!!

COMANCHE: Ice it down, Cross. Chill out, man!

CROSS: MAN, FUCK THIS INTERNAL AFFAIRS MOTHERFUCKER!!!

BOWIE: Ex-Internal Affairs. Past tense.

CROSS: Man, Comanche, you should be wanting a piece of his ass your own damn self. Punk bitch sold you out, and y'all supposed to be womb-to-tomb, back-to-back motherfuckers. Sold you out for thirty pieces of silver like you was a motherfucking stranger!

ROYAL BOY: Now that is definitely worth an ass whipping! Kick his ass, homes!

COMANCHE: That's on me, not on you, Superboy! Let it alone.

BOWIE: That's all right, Comanche. If Junior is feeling froggish, let him leap. He ain't nothing but a coffee break.

CROSS: I'll break my foot in your ass!

BOWIE: Then come on with it, punk! Bring your best shot! I ain't a little girl.

CROSS: MOTHERFUCKER!!!

COMANCHE: CROSS!!!

ROYAL BOY: COME ON, Y'ALL!!! LET'S GET IT ON!!! WILD WILD WEST!!!

BOWIE: I believe if you let the brother go, Comanche, he'll find a more profound way to express himself.

CROSS: LET ME GO, COMANCHE!!!

BOWIE: Let him go, Comanche!

ROYAL BOY: LET HIM GO, COMANCHE!!!

COMANCHE: SQUASH IT, MAN!!!

CROSS: I'M KICKING HIS ASS!!!

ROYAL BOY: `BOUT TIME SOMEBODY KICKED SOMEBODY'S ASS!!!

COMANCHE: SHUT UP!!!

(BABE RUTH *comes back into the Community Affairs room.*)

BABE RUTH: What in the Sam Hill is going on in here?

CROSS: I'M GONNA GET ME SOME OF THAT ITALIAN SUIT WEARING ASS!!!

BABE RUTH: OFFICER BEAUCHAMP!!! CHILL OUT, AND I MEAN NOW!!!

CROSS: IS THAT A DIRECT FUCKING ORDER?!!

BABE RUTH: AS DIRECT AS GOD TALKING TO MOSES, MOTHERFUCKER!!! CEASE AND DESIST RIGHT THE FUCK NOW!!! *(Silence)* Let him go. Bowie…what in the hell were you doing?

BOWIE: I didn't do a thing.

BABE RUTH: You were left in charge of this precinct. You were not expected to instigate a small-scale riot.

ROYAL BOY: Y'all some weak-kneed limps, man. You couldn't shake up a paranoid hypochondriac.

BABE RUTH: Please be quiet.

ROYAL BOY: *(Affecting an English accent)* "I say, old sport, that would be rather unthinkable. I'd much rather just patter on, and on, you know, chip, chip, chip, and a bowl of Cheerios, motherfucker!"

BABE RUTH: Cute.

COMANCHE: Caution, Royal Boy. Push can come to shove in a split second. Never underestimate your bad luck.

ROYAL BOY: Y'all ain't shit. A Police Boy would be fucking it up right about now.

COMANCHE: Thought you didn't know anything about the Police Boys?

ROYAL BOY: I've heard some rumors, baby.

COMANCHE: I bet you have.

ROYAL BOY: I know the history. The story in legend.
I know you faggots can't hang with the genuine shit,
brother.

BOWIE: Then you should know who you are talking
to, young blood. Comanche, myself, and your mentor
the Big Bad Bed started the Police Boys. We were the
original article, little brother.

COMANCHE: You forgot Cochise.

BOWIE: That's funny coming from you, Comanche,
because if my memory serves me correctly, you did.
But those days are gone. Different ways...different
days. We the law now. To protect and to serve, right?
We don't break the peace, we keep it, right?

COMANCHE: Right.

BOWIE: We don't break laws, we don't break heads...

COMANCHE: ALL RIGHT, DROP IT!!!

BOWIE: The stress isn't getting to you, is it, Comanche?

BABE RUTH: That's enough, Bowie.

BOWIE: Well, that is what they want me to keep a close
eye on, you know what I mean? With us being so close
over the years, who better to make sure that everything
is everything with our favorite knight in shining armor.

COMANCHE: Are you through?

BOWIE: With you? For now. I mean it isn't like you are
Cross the Superboy here, somebody who can't tell the
difference between being a gangster or a cop.

CROSS: Fuck you, punk! Keep it up, and I'll show you
the motherfucking difference, buddy!

BABE RUTH: THAT'S ENOUGH!!! ...Bowie, you've
been warned, I ain't gonna tell you again. Cross...what
is your problem?

CROSS: What's my problem?

BABE RUTH: You were being restrained by a fellow police officer from attacking another police officer.

CROSS: I ain't had no problem with it.

BABE RUTH: You might not have a problem with it, but you have been a problem with everybody else from the day you were born. Anybody who ever came in contact with you.

CROSS: At least I know how to watch somebody's back.

BABE RUTH: What are you saying?

CROSS: I think I said it.

BABE RUTH: I'm the one who doesn't watch somebody's back?

CROSS: You more interested in showing off your so-called superiority.

BABE RUTH: Wait a minute. Who in the hell's back have you ever covered?

CROSS: Goddammit, Babe, you know I can't stand a motherfucking feminist. If one was on fire, I wouldn't piss on her to save her life, but if that bitch was my partner, out in the jungle, I'd take a goddamned bullet between the eyes to save her life, and you know that's true. You know me, man.

BABE RUTH: Does that go for Republican feminists as well, or is this just a jack-ass kind of thing?

CROSS: That ain't what I'm talking about! Man, Comanche took a shotgun blast dead in the gut what was meant for me. Pulled me out of the way and didn't even flich. That's a motherfucking cop. You would have let my ass get blown the fuck away, and you know that's true, too. Behind some standard operating procedure bullshit. You gonna get somebody killed someday behind all your rinky dink by the book madness.

BABE RUTH: Really? Well as long as I don't have you on my back I'll probably live long and prosper.

CROSS: Me? What about you? You almost got me killed!

BABE RUTH: I almost got you killed?

COMANCHE: What are you yapping about now?

CROSS: I had to walk into some serious Little Big Horn action, in the heart of Police Boys territory, behind some stupidness Babe Ruth and Miller High Life got caught up in.

BABE RUTH: Go ahead. I wanna see how you gonna tell this lie.

COMANCHE: How you get caught in Little Big Horn?

CROSS: I was off duty, cruising the old Cut, and I peep Babe Ruth and Miller High Life in the middle of some real ugly turbulence between these two orangutan looking motherfuckers, and this brother the size of Cuba, leaning heavily against a partially open door, Babe and Miller looking like Little Bo Peep and her lost black sheep.

BABE RUTH: We saw some action, and were investigating same.

CROSS: No shit!

BABE RUTH: Standard operating…

CROSS: PROCEDURE!!! Yeah, well, calling yourself some goddamned backup is S O P, too, ya silly doofus G O P motherfucker!

BABE RUTH: Why didn't you call it?

CROSS: BECAUSE I WAS THE MOTHERFUCKING BACKUP, DAMMIT!!! I WAS THE BACKUP!!! I WAS SO BUSY WATCHING Y'ALL EXPOSE YOUR SHIT TO THE WORLD THAT I COULDN'T COVER MY OWN GODDAMN BACK!!! FUCKING CHILD

CARE!!! I walk up on all this nonsense on the front porch, not knowing nothing about nothing, but big and bold as I wanna be, and with weapon out in plain full view, go "What's up?" Cuba and the orangutans ain't into it. They say, "Get lost, ain't nobody call me". I say, "Fuck that, I ain't from Domino's Pizza, I'm a motherfucking cop, go the fuck where I want to go, and right now, I want to be here". BOOM!!! There it is. Me, the Girl Blunder and her Boy Friday stuck in the middle of some serious buzzed-out crackhead mess with only the Masada solution as a viable number two plan. I'm checking the orangutans, but they let Big Cuba get to his shit behind the door.

ROYAL BOY: They get you caught like that, and they can't cover your weak side? They couldn't watch your back?

CROSS: Man, those simple-ass niggers couldn't watch television.

ROYAL BOY: You should have broke and booked on they sorry asses.

CROSS: I'm hip!

(CROSS and ROYAL BOY slap hands.)

CROSS: WHAT THE FUCK AM I DOING TALKING TO YOU!!! (He kicks the cage.) SHUT UP!!!

COMANCHE: So what happened?

BABE RUTH: You want me to tell him, or can you finish the story truthfully?

CROSS: The truth is you and Miller High Life had no business up there!

BABE RUTH: You had no business up there! We had it under control!

BOWIE: Why don't you tell Comanche about what went down on the porch that day. It's the kind of story I just bet he'll understand.

CROSS: I've had about all I'm gonna motherfucking stand from you, punk!

COMANCHE: Will somebody tell me what in the hell happened on that porch?

ROYAL BOY: WAIT A MINUTE!!! I know who the hell you are, motherfucker! The Big Bad Bed and the Police Boys are gonna bust a million caps right up your asshole into your motherfucking soul! You punk ass nigger!

CROSS: Listen up, little nigger, I have a graveyard disposition...

ROYAL BOY: And a tombstone mind...

CROSS: I am the bad mother of motherfuckers...

ROYAL BOY: And you don't mind dying.

CROSS: I'm a true-blue, hope-to-die motherfucker, so don't think you can either sweat, slick, or punk me off! I will end the last days of your puberty, you hear me?

BABE RUTH: Cross, get away from the cage.

ROYAL BOY: You don't like being sweated?

CROSS: Just sweat me and find the fuck out!

BABE RUTH: CROSS!!!

(CROSS *turns to* BABE RUTH, ROYAL BOY *retrieves the drinking cup he pissed in and heads toward* CROSS.)

ROYAL BOY: Cheers, motherfucker!

(ROYAL BOY *throws the piss in* CROSS's *face*.)

ROYAL BOY: You should have opted for the sweat, brother.

(CROSS *leaps at the cage,* BABE RUTH *and* COMANCHE *grab him and pull him away.*)

ROYAL BOY: What...want a refill?

CROSS: I'm gonna break your crazy goddamn neck! I'm gonna kill you!

BOWIE: I don't know about you guys, but I am having a hell of a time. Y'all need some backup, or what?

BABE RUTH: Bowie, will you shut the hell up! You could help, you know!

COMANCHE: Cross! What in the hell is wrong with you?

CROSS: What in the hell is wrong with me? What in the hell is wrong with you? Talking all this lawyer nonsense bullshit like that is who you are!

COMANCHE: It is who I am!

CROSS: IT AIN'T WHO YOU WERE! YOU WERE A WARRIOR! I SHOULD KNOW BETTER THAN ANYBODY! YOU WERE THE FIRST ONE TO PICK UP A CALL, THE FIRST TO GO BUSTING THROUGH A DOOR, MAN, NOBODY HAD MORE BALLS, MORE HEART THAN YOU! NOW YOU DON'T EVEN CARRY A WEAPON!

COMANCHE: MAYBE I DON'T WANT TO! YOU EVER THINK ABOUT THAT?

CROSS: I THINK EVER SINCE YOU CRACKED THAT RED SKULL'S HEAD OPEN YOU BEEN BUGGING OUT SO SERIOUSLY I CAN'T EVEN RECOGNIZE YOU ANYMORE! YOU WERE THE LAST NIGGER I EVER THOUGHT WOULD GO SOFT ON ME, MAN!

COMANCHE: I WENT SOFT ON YOU?

CROSS: I'M SORRY, BROTHER, I CALLS THEM LIKE I SEES THEM!!!

COMANCHE: I MIGHT NOT BE WHAT YOU WANT ME TO BE ANYMORE, BUT AT LEAST I AM HERE FOR YOU!!!

CROSS: What's that supposed to mean?

COMANCHE: You ain't always been there for me, brother, have you? You so damn proud I took that shot gun blast for you, where the hell were you when I was in the hospital. I don't remember you coming by there to see how your hero was doing. I don't remember a phone call, a get well card, nothing.

CROSS: I didn't have the stomach to see you like that.

COMANCHE: I DIDN'T WANT TO BE LIKE THAT!!! FUCK WHAT YOU DIDN'T HAVE THE STOMACH TO LOOK AT, I ALMOST LOST MINE LOOKING OUT FOR YOU!!! *(Pause)* So, sorry if you can't understand why I feel the need to make some changes in the way I live my life, but to be honest and frank with you, little brother, you ain't got the right to question the shit I do.

(Silence)

BABE RUTH: Cross... Why don't you go and clean yourself off.

CROSS: Man...later for you, bitch!

(Beat)

BABE RUTH: What did you say to me?

ROYAL BOY: Man, later for you, bitch, and he said it like he meant it.

BABE RUTH: You had better never call me that shit again, if you know what's good for you. You hear me?

CROSS: What you gonna do? Fine my ass?

COMANCHE: Superboy, walk away, man, before...

BABE RUTH: Shut up, Comanche! I'll do more than fine you.

CROSS: You ain't nothing but a former desk jockey, teacher's politically correct pet, head of the class, penis envy motherfucking scavenging geechie bitch!

ROYAL BOY: POW!!!

BABE RUTH: I will walk your fresh-out-of-the-ghetto ass like the good Lord walked to Galilee!!!

ROYAL BOY: DOUBLE POW!!!

CROSS: THEN START WALKING!!! YOU WOULDN'T BE TALKING NO KIND OF SHIT IF A J WAS STILL ALIVE!!! IT WAS PROBABLY YOU AND YOUR SICK BULLSHIT THAT FINALLY HELPED DRIVE HIM OUT OF HIS MIND AND MADE HIM BLOW HIS BRAINS OUT!!!

ROYAL BOY: OUCH!!!

CROSS: YOU WOULDN'T BE GIVING NO KIND OF ORDERS, SAYING NOTHING TO NOBODY, ALL YOU GOT SAVING YOU FROM ME KICKING YOUR ASS RIGHT NOW IS YOUR TEMPORARY BULLSHIT MOTHERFUCKING RANK!!!

BABE RUTH: COME ON WITH IT, PUNK!!! I DON'T SEE ANY BRACES ON YOUR LEGS!!!

(CROSS leaps at BABE RUTH, who leaps right back at him. They go at it fiercely for a hot minute before COMANCHE and BOWIE can separate them.)

COMANCHE: KNOCK IT OFF!!! THE BOTH OF YOU!!! COME ON, BABE RUTH, YOU IN CHARGE!!!

BABE RUTH: LET ME GO!!!

BOWIE: YOU OKAY!!!

BABE RUTH: FINE!!! NEVER BETTER!!! LET ME GO, THAT'S AN ORDER!!!

(Everything settles down.)

ROYAL BOY: Woooww, man. That was like pretty exciting. Just like Dodge motherfucking City on a Saturday night, with gunfighters and everything.

COMANCHE: Just shut up, kid, alright?

ROYAL BOY: When's the next show? I got time to get some popcorn and shit?

COMANCHE: Shut up! You all right, Babe?

BABE RUTH: Yeah. Yeah, I'm fine.

COMANCHE: Cross?

CROSS: I'm okay.

COMANCHE: We all been doing this work for too damn long to come apart at the seams now. I know what's wrong. A J's suicide is messing with everybody's head. Everybody is so tight in here today they don't know whether to shit or wind their wrist watch. We are all under a lot of stress and...

BABE RUTH: Save me the pop psychology, Comanche, all right? If I am gonna ride Cross for jumping another police officer, the same rules have got to apply to me as well. This hasn't a thing to do with A J. It's got everything to do with us, and how we are gonna handle ourselves. No excuses.

COMANCHE: Whatever you say.

BABE RUTH: I don't need anybody to hold my hand. Neither does Cross.

COMANCHE: Okay.

BABE RUTH: Superboy, you cool.

CROSS: Like a milk shake.

BABE RUTH: Good. Talk to me like that again, and I will have you out of here so fast you'll get diabetes. You understand me?

CROSS: I understand you.

ROYAL BOY: I understand you too, baby. You should wrestle with me next time. I'll not only change your life, I'll change your mind.

BABE RUTH: And I have just about had all the mouth out of you that I care to stand. Bowie, tape his mouth shut and cuff him.

BOWIE: I can't do that.

BABE RUTH: I don't recall asking your permission.

ROYAL BOY: What y'all talking 'bout, some tape?

CROSS: I got it, Babe Ruth.

COMANCHE: Bowie's right, we can't do that. That's violating his rights.

BABE RUTH: I don't recall asking your opinion either.

COMANCHE: We ain't got the right to treat the boy that way.

ROYAL BOY: Watch my back, pretender!

BABE RUTH: Comanche, tread lightly. I'm done giving people rope for the day.

COMANCHE: He's a kid, not a dog.

BABE RUTH: He's the devil, Comanche! He ain't worth the dirt I scrape from the bottom of my shoe at night.

COMANCHE: He is a human being!

BABE RUTH: He is a rabid animal! You don't do something about him soon and he will infect the entire community! We already have whole neighborhoods full of crazed mad dogs like him foaming at the mouth destroying decent human beings, that need to be put out of their misery.

COMANCHE: Like it or not, he still belongs to us...

BABE RUTH: I don't claim him! Just read this hospital report of another human being who got in his way, and see if you can find his compassion or humanity. Go ahead! Then we'll discuss your theories after you digested it. I'll be interested to hear what you have to say then. BOWIE!!!

BOWIE: Yes?

BABE RUTH: Go make us some coffee.

BOWIE: Why do I gotta...

BABE RUTH: MOTHERFUCKER DO YOU OUTRANK ME!!!

BOWIE: No.

BABE RUTH: Then do the fuck like I say.

(BOWIE *goes over to the coffee pot and begins to make the coffee.* FELLOWS *enters.*)

FELLOWS: Why is the kid bound and gagged?

BABE RUTH: A quiet Community Affairs room is a happy Community Affairs room.

FELLOWS: Ungag him.

BABE RUTH: That's a negative.

FELLOWS: We'll see about that. Where's Jabali?

BABE RUTH: None of your business. I have command until he gets back.

FELLOWS: Really?

BABE RUTH: Really.

(Beat)

FELLOWS: I have the boy's L R A downstairs. His mother.

BABE RUTH: I'll come down with you.

FELLOWS: You'll come down with me?

BABE RUTH: Keep you honest. Nothing more. I'm going with Fellows to talk to the thing's alleged mother.

(Suddenly we hear a burst of gunshots and windows exploding. Everybody hits the deck. We hear a car screeching off and then there is quiet. During the volley of bullets, ROYAL BOY has worked his hands from behind his back and taken off the tape.)

ROYAL BOY: *(Childlike)* Who's afraid of the Big Bad Bed, the Big Bad Bed, the Big Bad Bed. Who's afraid of the Big Bad Bed... *(Darkly)* Every-motherfucking-body in here.

(THE SIGNIFYING MONKEY comes over to COMANCHE, who feels his presence.)

THE SIGNIFYING MONKEY: Are you prepared for me?

COMANCHE: I am trying.

THE SIGNIFYING MONKEY: Have you done all I have asked of you to become the truth?

COMANCHE: I don't know. I'm trying, but I don't know what you want.

THE SIGNIFYING MONKEY: You must first travel to the center of your own demons, and go live inside of the soul of the beast.

COMANCHE: But I...

THE SIGNIFYING MONKEY: And remember...he who does not search, will not find.

(Lights back up on the Community Affairs room. COMANCHE and ROYAL BOY are alone, COMANCHE reading a book titled Voodoo Contra.)

ROYAL BOY: Hey, brother!

COMANCHE: What do you want, man?

ROYAL BOY: Some wild-ass shit, huh?

COMANCHE: Some stupid shit.

ROYAL BOY: Come on, that move was bold like a motherfucker! Pulling a drive-by on Pig Heaven! You better tell these fools that the Big Bad Bed don't play.

COMANCHE: Why don't you tell the Captain yourself?

ROYAL BOY: Nice try, Clyde. But I ain't telling that nigger nothing but fairy tales. *(Pause)* So what was it like? Between you and me?

COMANCHE: What was what like?

ROYAL BOY: What was it like being one of the original Police Boys?

COMANCHE: It wasn't anything special.

ROYAL BOY: Come on, brother blood. Word on the bricks was that y'all was like the real treacherous legendary shit, you know what I'm saying?

COMANCHE: Nothing legendary about it.

ROYAL BOY: That ain't what I heard?

COMANCHE: Don't believe everything you hear.

ROYAL BOY: At least tell me why you and Bogart went from being for real original gangsters to the state of confusion you in now?

COMANCHE: You think we're confused?

ROYAL BOY: You tell me. You gone from being Police Boys to being Five-O. You gone from Down For The Hood, to being New Jack Night-Riding patterollers. Come on, bleed, you and me both from the Cut. How could y'all walk away from it all, and step on the Big Bad Bed like that, man?

COMANCHE: And live?

ROYAL BOY: Yeah…well, that too. Come on, cuz, tell me a bedtime story.

(Silence)

COMANCHE: Well...we were lost inside of the world alone except for each other. We were orphans. My family sent me out of Nigeria during the Civil War. Bowie was from Cuba. They say they found the Big Bad Bed in the streets in a pool of blood. Both Bowie and I were so young when we crossed different waters to get here we couldn't remember our families at all. Not a single image. All we had was a name, Chileogus for me, Santiago for Bowie. Later when we got our adoptive names, we kept our family names as middle names trying not to forget what we couldn't recall. The Big Bad Bed didn't even have that. All he knew was that he wasn't wanted, that he was thrown away, worse than garbage. Even garbage has a place to be, you know what I'm saying?

ROYAL BOY: Yeah, I know what you saying.

COMANCHE: Maybe that's why the Bed has always been a little off. Anyways, once upon a time there was four amigos.

ROYAL BOY: Four? Who's the fourth motherfucker?

COMANCHE: Cochise. He was the leader. Nobody knew where he came from. We were tough, and hard, but we had honor. We ran our neighborhood, just the four of us, and protected it with our fists. It might not have been the best way to come up, but it was the only option we had. The Bed got into some serious whacked out assault and battery thing, and got sent to the slams. The nature of the gang changed. We started to get political, you know, trying to get free lunch, and breakfast going for the neighborhood kids, and shit. Things like that. Cochise believed we had to evolve to a higher plane. Well...one day whilst Cochise, Bowie and me were playing some cutthroat basketball, we make out this brother coming at us from across the playground. It was the Bed. He had some partners with him. Cochise runs over to him. Arms wide open, ready to welcome the brother back into the fold. Bed took out a pistol, and put three bullets into his face. One of his partners had made their way around me and Bowie and took Bowie out quick with a pistol whip to the head. He then stuck his pistol right in Bowie's unconscious ear, and pulled back the hammer. The Bed said times had changed, and the Police Boys had grown soft with all this political bullshit. Talk was cheap, and a nigger that ain't ready to kill had better be ready to die. The world had gotten hard, and we had to follow the times. For old times sake, he was gonna let us walk away if we didn't see eye to eye but I had to give him my word that me and Bowie would walk away clean, no payback, or he would have Bowie's brains blown out through his ears. I told him, you want it, you got it. It's your world, and I don't want to be living in it. I promised him both of us would leave the Cut, and no vengeance would be coming back at him from either of us over Cochise.

ROYAL BOY: You're kidding me? The Big Bad Bed let it play out like that?

COMANCHE: It was an honor thing. There was a time when that meant something in the neighborhood. Even to the Big Bad Bed. Bowie kept my word, no matter how much he hated it. We both entered the Marines, but went our separate ways after that. I guess he felt I had no right compromising his honor, even if it saved his life. Somehow we both became cops, and...well let's just say payback is a bitch, Bowie got some with me, and let us leave it at that.

ROYAL BOY: Hey, man, I can understand the nigger. Didn't you want a piece of the Big Bad Bed behind your partner getting blanked?

COMANCHE: We were all partners. Now, we ain't shit. What's the point?

(JABALI, BABE RUTH, CROSS, *and* BOWIE *enter.*)

ROYAL BOY: HEY!! DON'T ANYBODY WANT TO HEAR ABOUT MY MIS-SPENT YOUTH?!!

JABALI: Comanche! Into my office!

ROYAL BOY: ANYBODY KNOW ANY CHAIN GANG SONGS?!!

(JABALI *closes the door to his office after everybody enters.*)

JABALI: I just left Royal Boy's mother. She won't be a problem. She just wants him to go somewhere where they can do him the most good.

CROSS: How does she feel about the penitentiary?

JABALI: Five dollars, Superboy.

CROSS: What did I say? I didn't say nothing.

JABALI: Stupid remarks are just as offensive to my ears.

(CROSS *pays* JABALI.)

COMANCHE: What was the mother like?

JABALI: A junkie flunking out of a halfway house. She was afraid we were gonna put her back in stir. She'll do anything we want.

COMANCHE: She might not hold up in a court of law as his L R A. Counsel will say she compromised his rights. I wouldn't bet too much on that horse. We should get counsel in here as soon as possible, and accept no confession if we can get it out of him beforehand.

JABALI: You sure about that?

COMANCHE: Why take the risk? See if you can finagle a woman P D. Macho as he is, five will get you ten he'll either scare the shit out of her, or she'll piss him off, and he'll reject her.

JABALI: And that might give us some more time to get him to give up the Bed?

COMANCHE: Worth a shot.

JABALI: Okay. Babe Ruth? I have a request from the Sheriff's department to give them somebody experienced to help corral all the negative energy that's out on the streets. It's the day after the elections, and the Big Bad Bed and the Police Boys are making like the Corleone Family run by Al Capone.

BABE RUTH: You want me to run A J's old drill, right?

JABALI: Right. You'll need a shotgun rider. Take Cross.

BABE RUTH: I'd rather have Comanche, sir.

JABALI: And the devil wants ice water, but you will take Cross the Superboy, and that's an order. Comanche is on desk duty. End of discussion.

BABE RUTH: Yes sir.

JABALI: But before you go out, something is waiting for me down in evidence. I want you to bring it to me before you and Superboy hit the bricks. You follow me?

BABE RUTH: Yes sir. Just stay clear of me, Cross. I want to die of old age.

CROSS: Shoot. Stick with me and you'll live forever.

(They exit.)

JABALI: Comanche, the kid. I think we have a gold mine with him.

COMANCHE: He's smart as a whip, and a master manipulator. He had us eating out of his hand, and he was just scatting the riff.

JABALI: Smart and bold is a bad combination in his predicament. Makes you get sloppy. Think you can do no wrong. We'll let him talk. Maybe he'll say something.

(FELLOWS *comes in seething.*)

FELLOWS: Jabali!

JABALI: What can I do for you, counselor?

FELLOWS: Did I misrepresent myself to you earlier? Did you not understand what I was saying?

JABALI: I haven't the foggiest idea what you're talking about.

FELLOWS: The mother! I wanted to talk to her!

JABALI: Didn't you?

FELLOWS: Please do not give me that shit, Jabali! I come up here to inform you that I have her downstairs, all hell breaks loose, and then when I get back downstairs, she can't be found, but I find out while I'm looking for her, you have spirited her away, and interviewed her.

JABALI: You want my notes?

FELLOWS: I told you already the Governor told me I don't have to put up with any of your shit.

JABALI: We all can't have a warm and understanding relationship with the Governor like you, counselor.

FELLOWS: The Governor is not pleased with your progress with the gangs. He wants them eradicated.

JABALI: Especially because they're black.

FELLOWS: Oh no, please. That's a very, very tired argument.

JABALI: Really. That isn't what has brought you down to us with, shall we say, extreme prejudice?

FELLOWS: Really? Have you forgotten about Estelene Raye? Even the Royal Boy remembers her.

JABALI: My men were blown away by what happened to her, and admittedly in their zealous desire to apprehend the perpetrators...

FELLOWS: They were sloppy gathering evidence at the scene of the crime, and acted as if they hadn't a thimbleful of knowledge about proper procedure.

JABALI: THEY WERE BLOWN AWAY!!!

FELLOWS: WE HAD THE BIG BAD BED. WE HAD HIM COLD AND DEAD TO RIGHTS AND WE HAD TO LET HIM WALK AWAY CLEAN. WHY? BECAUSE YOUR MEN FUCKED THE CASE!!!

JABALI: THEY WERE BLOWN AWAY!!! HOW WOULD YOU HAVE FELT...

FELLOWS: I DID FEEL!!! I FELT SO SICK TO MY STOMACH ABOUT WHAT HAPPENED... *(Pause)* Your men saw her that day. I have been seeing her every night since in my dreams. I can't stop seeing her, her face smashed into a pulp, her arms and legs were broken into a hundred pieces, and her right hand was hacked off and stuffed in what was left of her mouth. I can't stop seeing that poor girl because I can't get it out of my system that we failed her. All of us. And, yes, Estelene Raye was black.

JABALI: We will do our job. No more mistakes.

FELLOWS: Yeah, well, I'm going to see to it that you do. I do not want you interrogating that boy without me present. You just had a cop commit suicide, now you've got one cop in your unit with a bad shot, and another just coming back from the bug house for smashing a kid's head in.

JABALI: It says on the final report on both cases self-defense.

FELLOWS: Well we know what it says and what it is are two different things. Aren't I right Sergeant Bowie?

BOWIE: Don't ask me. I just make the coffee around here.

FELLOWS: Don't go south on me now, too. I want you to keep an eye on things in here, understand? By the way, Captain, he isn't a peewee anymore. He just graduated, and Proposition 13 passed last night, just in time for the Royal Boy.

(Silence)

JABALI: We can use that. Comanche…bring the Royal Boy.

COMANCHE: Yes sir.

BOWIE: And what do you want me to do?

JABALI: Just do what you do best.

(COMANCHE brings in ROYAL BOY.)

JABALI: Now, let us resume our little chat.

ROYAL BOY: Fine with me. How you doing, girlfriend. Long time no see.

FELLOWS: We're going to have a lot of time to get reacquainted.

JABALI: Again, why do you think we brought you in last night, your Royal Badness?

ROYAL BOY: How would I know?

FELLOWS: Really?

ROYAL BOY: I was just prancing the bricks, baby. Getting into that fresh air kind of thing, you know what I'm saying?

BOWIE: That it?

ROYAL BOY: For real. Why? What's on y'all's pee butt minds?

JABALI: A question. Something simple. We were just trying to figure out what you were doing following that woman.

(Pause)

ROYAL BOY: What woman?

JABALI: Oh, we have witnesses who know something about you, and this woman. Just can't wait to talk to a grand jury about it, too.

COMANCHE: I think you better get that lawyer before you say anything else.

BOWIE: That's of course if you think the situation is getting beyond what you can handle.

ROYAL BOY: I can handle anything you punks throw down. I don't need me a lawyer for y'all's bullshit. I ain't done nothing to no woman, man. I already told you that.

JABALI: I don't recall anybody ever asking you.

FELLOWS: But thanks for letting us know she's on your mind.

ROYAL BOY: So I remember seeing some kind of woman. So the fuck what?

FELLOWS: Better not say anything without legal representation.

COMANCHE: For your own good.

BOWIE: Might trip over your own tongue with all these lies you're telling.

ROYAL BOY: Take your best shot, chumps! We seen this woman jogging.

JABALI: Where?

ROYAL BOY: The Square by Circle Park.

JABALI: What time was all of this happening, this watching?

ROYAL BOY: How should I know? I ain't got a watch.

BOWIE: Thought big time gangsters like you kept them fifty watches.

ROYAL BOY: Had a going out of business sale.

JABALI: You want us to tell you what time it was?

BOWIE: Your Royal Sadness?

ROYAL BOY: Fuck you, man! I don't like you!

JABALI: Not many people do. The woman, Royal Boy, what about the woman?

ROYAL BOY: Look, the bitch just stumbled into some alleyway, heaving, throwing up, and shit. She was crying and snotting like she was some little lost baby weeping in the rain. Imagine that.

JABALI: I am.

ROYAL BOY: I ain't touched her, man. That's the straight dope.

FELLOWS: Who did?

ROYAL BOY: I don't know. I left her there.

FELLOWS: I bet you did.

BOWIE: Sure you're not forgetting something?

ROYAL BOY: Man, forget you, alright?

COMANCHE: Everything you telling us happened the way you say it happened?

FELLOWS: You're not leaving anything out?

BOWIE: Your mind like a sheet of glass, huh?

ROYAL BOY: That's right, crystal motherfucking clear and clean.

JABALI: You sure about that?

ROYAL BOY: Ain't that what I said? What? Y'all can't understand English?

(BABE RUTH *and* CROSS *come back into* JABALI'*s office with a sack.*)

JABALI: Counselor, can we talk to his Royal Badness, heart to heart, alone for a hot minute?

FELLOWS: Sure. I'll be downstairs, checking on his defender. *(Exits)*

JABALI: You haven't left anything out?

ROYAL BOY: Not a single thing.

JABALI: Then maybe you can explain to me what I have in this sack?

ROYAL BOY: What?

JABALI: CATCH!!!

(JABALI *throws something at* ROYAL BOY *from out of the sack.*)

ROYAL BOY: GET THIS MESS OFF ME!!!

JABALI: IT'S THE WOMAN'S SWEAT SUIT!!!

BOWIE: THE ONE IN THE ALLEY!!!

JABALI: REMEMBER? But it's not covered in vomit, it's covered in blood!

BOWIE: Her blood!

COMANCHE: Who was with you, Royal Boy?

BOWIE: Where was the Big Bad Bed?

COMANCHE: Help yourself out, brother!

BOWIE: You gonna talk, talk!

BABE RUTH: Cause I got some good news and some bad news for you, punk!

ROYAL BOY: What news?

BABE RUTH: The bad news is that the woman died!

ROYAL BOY: WHAT?!!

BOWIE: The good news is that we got your shiny little behind stone cold for the deed!

ROYAL BOY: YOU'RE LYING!!!

JABALI: You're going to get charged with murder one!

BABE RUTH: We got witnesses!

BOWIE: White witnesses!

CROSS: White witnesses? Oh, you in big trouble now.

ROYAL BOY: THERE WEREN'T NOBODY AROUND, YOU MOTHERFUCKING LIE!!!

JABALI: You know that because you were there?

COMANCHE: You were just helping her out?

BABE RUTH: When you left her she was alive and well?

ROYAL BOY: Right, alive, right!

BOWIE: Just a little vomit, but alive, right?

ROYAL BOY: Right! I ain't killed nobody, man!

BABE RUTH: You just raped her.

BOWIE: But didn't kill her.

JABALI: Right?

ROYAL BOY: Right—NO! FUCK YOU, MAN, I AIN'T GOTTA SIT HERE AND...

JABALI: SIT DOWN!!!

BOWIE: She's dead, buddy. She's as dead as she is ever gonna be.

BABE RUTH: There was a lot of blood.

BOWIE: A whole lot of blood! Whew!

BABE RUTH: School's out, junior!

JABALI: We have the knife, the rock we found in the knife's handle, you have admitted to following the woman, placed yourself at the scene of the crime, admitted to raping the woman…

ROYAL BOY: I AIN'T RAPED NOBODY!!! YOU ALL TRICKED ME INTO SAYING THAT!!! I WANT A LAWYER, MAN!!!

BOWIE: Getting a little too hot to handle?

BABE RUTH: I don't know if a lawyer is gonna be enough.

BOWIE: You gonna need Abraham Lincoln to set your butt free.

JABALI: Book him! Make sure his Mommy and a pretender gets to talk to him before you pitch him under the jail. Murder in the first degree with all the trimmings. You know what that is, don't you? You watch television, right? Cheer up. You have finally made the Big Show! Ain't no stopping you now. You are an original gangster! A Police Boy! This interview is over, your Royal Badness!

(The phone rings. JABALI answers it.)

JABALI: Ninety-ninth Precinct. Captain Jabali LaRouche speaking. *(Silence)* Thank you. *(He hangs up.)*

BABE RUTH: What is it, Captain?

COMANCHE: Captain?

JABALI: It was a doctor. From the hospital. My son's heart has stopped.

(A hush falls over the room as JABALI stares through ROYAL BOY.)

JABALI: Bad luck. Bad luck for everybody.

(THE SIGNIFYING MONKEY approaches the audience.)

THE SIGNIFYING MONKEY:
I found something in the night
Something the wind don't know

And a train whistle cannot blow
No clothes can clothe what I am not
or save me from the death of night
And the dark laughter of God
A craziness fills my blind eyes
with blood and strife
And though it's time for a break
Remember
There are no intermissions in American life.

(Lights fade to black.)

END OF ACT ONE

ACT TWO

Scene One

(Lights come up on the Community Affairs room. THE
SIGNIFYING MONKEY *is over* COMANCHE *who appears to be
in a trance.)*

THE SIGNIFYING MONKEY:
Now the Lion came back more dead than alive
That's when the Monkey started more of his signifying
    jive!
Saying "King of the Jungle, ain't you a bitch,
Look like your mama gave you crabs,
And the seven year itch,
Lightning must have struck you, and your bell's been
    rung
You smell like something that's been damn near hung!
WHOOP! There it is, motherfucker, don't you roar!
Or I'll jump out of this tree and whip your ass some
    more!
Cuz you a chickenshit pretender, your heart is void
    and null,
You can't build your house from the blood of a skull!

(Lights come up on ROYAL BOY *and* LADY IN WHITE.*)*

THE SIGNIFYING MONKEY: The Big Bad Bed say you
done took your ass whipping like a man, you have
shown you got heart. Now we gotta see what you can
do when you on the solo by your lonesome. Take her
off, then take her out. Ain't no pity in this city. We'll

play chickie for you outside the ally, and keep the coast clear.

(The LADY IN WHITE *tries to make a move to get away.* ROYAL BOY *puts a knife to her throat.*)

ROYAL BOY: BITCH BE COOL!! (*Silence*) You see, baby, I know all about some pounding and bumping titties with a motherfucker. Man, somedays I'd rather blow a motherfucker's brain the fuck out of his head than get some fine virgin pussy, my mother's love, or be the motherfucking President of the United fucking States, you hear what I'm saying? The only time you got the like for real true power in this bullshit motherfucking world is when you got somebody down on their knees, begging you for their life, calling on Jesus, ready to suck your dick, anything, rather than die. Think I'm lying? AM I BORING YOU BITCH?!!

LADY IN WHITE: I'm not going to beg you for anything. Not my life, not for anything. I'm not afraid of you. I'm not…

ROYAL BOY: SHUT THE MOTHERFUCK UP!!! (*Pause*) You see, bitch, the Wild Bunch is gonna ride tonight. I gotta tear through your soul to get my badge and become a true Police Boy, and leave all my childish things behind. So you might as well kick back, and enjoy the motherfucking ride.

(The lights go out on ROYAL BOY and LADY IN WHITE, and come back up on COMANCHE and THE SIGNIFYING MONKEY.)

COMANCHE: DON'T UNDO ME!

THE SIGNIFYING MONKEY: Ain't you heard, there ain't no use in you trying, cuz can't nobody stop this monkey from signifying!

(Lights change abruptly, and COMANCHE startles awake.)

ROYAL BOY: Hey, whaddup, man?

COMANCHE: What?

ROYAL BOY: You was down for the count, man.

COMANCHE: Must have dozed off or something.

ROYAL BOY: You was sweating, eyes wide open, you know what I'm saying?

COMANCHE: Yeah?

ROYAL BOY: I ain't ripping you, brother. You was like seeing something that no other motherfucker could see. I know I ain't seen it.

COMANCHE: You sound concerned.

ROYAL BOY: I don't want you bugging out on me, or nothing.

COMANCHE: I see.

ROYAL BOY: Besides, you a Police Boy. I know you gonna look out for me.

COMANCHE: That was another life, kid.

ROYAL BOY: Yeah, well, once a Police Boy always a Police Boy, you know what I'm saying? *(Silence)* Hey, man. You been reading that shit all motherfucking day.

COMANCHE: It helps sometimes.

ROYAL BOY: You really off into some voodoo and shit, huh? Run me down something about it. Enlighten me.

COMANCHE: You serious?

ROYAL BOY: Yeah.

COMANCHE: What's your name?

ROYAL BOY: Billy. What's yours?

COMANCHE: Chris.

ROYAL BOY: Well, come on, Chris, break out the word.

COMANCHE: Well, I guess the first thing about it that's interesting is that in the voodoo reality...

THE SIGNIFYING MONKEY: ...a person has nine souls.

ROYAL BOY: Shit...a motherfucker need at least that many these days.

COMANCHE: Each soul has a force and a personality which deals with a particular aspect of life in the world. Something that you have no choice but to ritualize.

ROYAL BOY: Talk motherfucking Engligh, man!

COMANCHE: It's like acting something out over and over, again and again.

ROYAL BOY: Alright, I gotcha. What these souls be?

COMANCHE: You got your soul that binds you to the rest of the universe, a soul that ties you to the human race, one that joins you to your race, fastens you to your sex, your nationality, let's see, your ancestors, your place in history...

THE SIGNIFYING MONKEY: ...your astral self...

ROYAL BOY: My what?

COMANCHE: Your astral self. It's about your particular talent. Your astral soul is what determines whether you're a farmer, or a mystic, or a warrior...

ROYAL BOY: Or a killer?

COMANCHE: Your spiritual magnetism can lead you to violence or tranquility.

ROYAL BOY: Go on, bleed.

COMANCHE: Well, your last soul is your personal soul. The soul of destiny. It connects and controls your life. Motivates and limits it. It writes out your entire life.

ROYAL BOY: Nothing you can do about it?

COMANCHE: Try as you might.

ROYAL BOY: Fucking figures.

COMANCHE: Yeah, I know.

(Pause)

ROYAL BOY: You read a lot, huh?

COMANCHE: Yeah.

ROYAL BOY: You ever read about the Silver Surfer?

COMANCHE: I'm not hip.

ROYAL BOY: Man, he had all of them souls you were talking about.

COMANCHE: No shit?

ROYAL BOY: Oh. Yeah, man. The Silver Surfer was like a classic comic book hero from the motherfucking Golden Age, brother. He was the bomb shit.

COMANCHE: He was down, huh?

ROYAL BOY: Aw, man, he was this great superhero, with strange and wonderful powers, but he had lost his memory. He had amnesia. He walked around the truly fucked of, like, humanity and shit, but he didn't know his real self. His powers, who he was, nothing. He couldn't remember a thing about that bullshit. Couldn't remember his nine souls from a baseball team. Honkies dogged his ass so bad he only thought he was what they thought he was.

COMANCHE: What was that?

ROYAL BOY: You know, some kind of wino, junkie, deviate, homeless motherfucker. He slept under the parking ramps, ate out of dumpsters, even took to putting white folks' throwaway garbage and shit on his body like trash was, like, charms or something.

COMANCHE: This sounds vaguely familiar.

ROYAL BOY: He just blended into the shit, and his memory grew out of all of that.

COMANCHE: He became the waste he moved throughout?

ROYAL BOY: The motherfucker was like unaware of the prince that he truly was.

COMANCHE: He was a prince?

ROYAL BOY: The nigger was the original Royal Boy, man. He was a prince of the forgotten blood and nobody could see it. The ruler of the lost great underwater kingdom of Atlantis. He was the invincible and magnificent Prince Namor, the son of the God of the Sea...

COMANCHE: Wait a minute, I know this comic book hero.

ROYAL BOY: You know the Silver Surfer?

COMANCHE: I know the Sub-Mariner.

ROYAL BOY: So fucking what, man?

COMANCHE: Prince Namor was the Sub-Mariner.

ROYAL BOY: What the fuck are you talking about?

COMANCHE: He tried to commit suicide by throwing himself into the sea. But the waters brought back his memory of who he was, and he took a mighty vengeance, wreaking havoc on all mankind. I remember this now.

ROYAL BOY: You saying the motherfucker wasn't the Silver Surfer?

COMANCHE: Prince Namor was the Sub-Mariner. I don't know who was the Silver Surfer.

ROYAL BOY: I don't believe that bullshit.

COMANCHE: Believe what you want. I know what I know.

ROYAL BOY: All right, man, if Prince Namor ain't the Silver Surfer, then answer me this.

COMANCHE: What?

ROYAL BOY: Where'd he get the surf board? *(Beat)* You can't answer that shit, can you?

COMANCHE: He didn't have a surf board.

ROYAL BOY: If he didn't have a surf board, then how did he get around in the water, man, since you know so fucking much?

COMANCHE: He had wings on his ankles, I don't know, he just swam.

ROYAL BOY: He swam with wings on his feet? You are about the dumbest sonuvabitch on the face of the planet, you know that shit, brother?

COMANCHE: I'm through with it, all right?

ROYAL BOY: Next you gonna tell me they called him the Sub-Mariner because he walked around with a submarine under his funky armpits...

COMANCHE: That wasn't what I was saying...

ROYAL BOY: You bugging out, brother...

COMANCHE: Who gives a shit, anyways? It was just a comic book hero. Kid shit!

ROYAL BOY: FUCK YOU AND YOUR KID SHIT!!! WEREN'T YOU THAT MOTHERFUCKER THAT WENT CRAZY, AND SMASHED THAT RED SKULL'S HEAD...

COMANCHE: ENOUGH, ALL RIGHT!!!

ROYAL BOY: THAT WHAT YOUR PERSONAL MOTHERFUCKING SOUL WROTE OUT FOR YOU?!!

COMANCHE: THAT'S IT!!! I AIN'T GONNA SAY IT AGAIN!!!

(Silence)

ROYAL BOY: Hey, man.

COMANCHE: I ain't in the mood.

ROYAL BOY: Why'd you do it?

COMANCHE: I ain't playing with you, keep it up, hear?

ROYAL BOY: I ain't dragging you, money. I ain't tricking.

COMANCHE: Why you so serious all of a sudden?

ROYAL BOY: Shit, man. I was born into the serious, you know what I'm saying?

COMANCHE: Yeah. Yeah, I know exactly what that reality is.

ROYAL BOY: Straight up truth. Give me the serum. Why you somersault out and waste that Skull like that, brother?

COMANCHE: Why do you want to know?

ROYAL BOY: Reasons for every season, brother blood. I don't know. I just gotta know, you know?

COMANCHE: I don't have any answers…what's your name again?

ROYAL BOY: Billy. Come on, man, you ain't got answers, rub some of them questions on me, man.

COMANCHE: I gotta lot of those.

ROYAL BOY: So run it down.

(Pause)

COMANCHE: I don't know. You know about what happened to Estelene Raye, right?

ROYAL BOY: I had nothing to do with that, man! I don't wanna hear it…

COMANCHE: I ain't saying that.

ROYAL BOY: No kind of ways!

COMANCHE: I'm the one who found her! Me and
Bowie...found her. *(Pause)* Found her that morning. It
was...you know what I'm saying?

ROYAL BOY: Yeah.

COMANCHE: What the Bed did to her...it was some
bizarre, surreal, sick shit, you know what I'm saying?
Later that night I started driving around. Driving just
to be driving. Trying to clear my head. Run out of gas,
fill it back up. Gotta keep driving. The picture of her
body lying in all of that blood kept playing over and
over in my mind. Like a ritual of horror. I just couldn't
shake the picture out of my mind, you know?

ROYAL BOY: Yeah.

COMANCHE: All of a sudden this kid comes running
out right in front of my car. Looked like a deer caught
in the headlights. I thought I hit him. I jumped out of
the car to check him out. I don't need this shit to be
happening, you know what I'm saying? I check him
out, and...man...I see he is all covered with blood. But
it ain't his blood. No, it was something else. He was
shaking like he was in a seizure, this silent screaming
in his eyes, his arm pointing to this old bombed-out
building. Pointing so hard it look like his arm was
gonna come right off and fly straight into that building.
This was just what I needed. Some righteous action,
right? I transformed myself into a dark avenging
angel before that kid's eyes, and I found myself
rushing headlong into that building like a makeshift
motherfucking juiced up Superman. But I wasn't
interested in truth, justice, or the American way. I
wanted payback for Estelene, Cochise, payback for my
whole entire fucking life. I got my weapon drawn, and
cocked, two hands on the pistol, following the smell
of violence. Turned a corner... and then I see it. Some
hopped-up, dusted out of his mind brother sporting

the colors of the Red Skulls just shooting at some little
child. He was just pulling the trigger, over and over
again. But the gun was empty. He had unloaded an
entire clip into this little child, who wasn't nothing but
a mass of blood, I couldn't even tell if the child was a
boy or a girl, she was so shot to shit. He couldn't even
tell he was out of bullets he was so high. I remember
that he was…humming or whistlin', or something
that started my blood boiling right inside my veins. I
screamed, "FREEZE MOTHERFUCKER!!!" He stopped
instantly and turned and looked directly into my eyes.
Then he smiled. The sonuvabitch smiled in my face.
He dropped his gun. I thought I heard him say, "Come
on and arrest me nigger. Come on and get you another
coonskin scalp for your old master. You can't touch
me. Ain't no crime in killing a nigger. See, a nigger
ain't worth shit. You don't believe me? Then watch
this." And he unzipped his pants, took out his thing,
and begun to… all over that poor little precious child.
And the nigger started to laugh. Right in my face. A
laugh that throbbed in my head, it seemed like for four
hundred years. A laugh that sucked all the belief in the
light, or love of God right out of my body, right out of
my soul, and filled me up with a darkness that would
scare Jesus from off of the cross. It slapped me back
into the world like a baby being born. I dropped my
gun, and took out my nightstick. A much more suitable
weapon for what I had in mind. That nigger stopped
laughing then, and just about turned white when he
saw the smile that crept onto my face. I transformed
into something that I still haven't words to describe.
Something the devil wouldn't claim. I brought the
stick down on top of his head, over and over, again
and again, until his head was no longer flesh covering
bone, but just this red mess. Looked kind of funny.
Like he had a head full of red hair. Wet red hair. I think
he only had time to scream one time.

ROYAL BOY: Shit.

COMANCHE: I called it in, then went home and took a shower. When they found me I was in the shower shaving. Only I wasn't shaving. I was slashing the shit out of my face. I was trying to cut my memory from out of my head. They told me when they found me I was talking in tongues.

ROYAL BOY: Goddamn, man, how did you feel?

COMANCHE: Content, man. For the moment.

ROYAL BOY: That's some intense shit, man.

COMANCHE: It still scares the living hell out of me.

ROYAL BOY: What the fuck for?

COMANCHE: I tasted his blood, Billy.

ROYAL BOY: So?

COMANCHE: I tasted his blood on my tongue, can't you understand anything?

ROYAL BOY: Fuck that scandalous motherfucker. He found out you weren't no joke. You should have beat his mama and daddy's ass too, you know what I'm saying?

COMANCHE: It wasn't just his blood, Billy. It was mine, too. His blood and my blood was all mixed up together. You understand what I'm saying?

ROYAL BOY: No, speak English, motherfucker!

COMANCHE: My blood, his blood, it was all the same. That's why it tasted so good to me. I wasn't beating him to death, I was swinging on everything I ever knew. I had become like a vampire that had developed a taste for his own blood. Needed to suck myself dry to stay alive. Shit, it was too easy, man. Killing a motherfucker was so simple, and it could take care of so much.

ROYAL BOY: I'm hip. That's the real dope there for your ass.

COMANCHE: But it can't take care of anything, Billy. It doesn't solve anything. You just walk the night deader than a zombie until you're lucky enough to have somebody return the favor and put you out of your misery. It's not the answer.

ROYAL BOY: So who gives a shit?

COMANCHE: You gotta give a shit, Billy! Don't you get it? You gotta give a damn about life and death, right or wrong, love and hate, or you are lost. Lost into a black hole of the darkest forever you ever gonna know. Not even the Wizard of Oz will be able to get you back home.

ROYAL BOY: So what the fuck is home? Man, forget all of that bullshit. We living at the end of the rainbow, brother. Ain't no pot of gold happening there for no niggers neither. Shit, we marching towards the apocalypse, some people gonna get smoked, some gonna do the smoking. Me, I'm gonna be one of the all time roasters of motherfuckers that there ever was. Shit, bring on doomsday, man! Bring on Armageddon! Bring on Satan and his weak-ass-faggot damnation! I ain't with none of that burning in hell bullshit! The motherfucker who is standing at the end when all the shit clears is the only winner! Niggers gotta get vicious like a motherfucker and quit taking ass whippings, or we gonna keep getting chewed up, spit out, and flushed down the toilet like we wasn't never here! That's what time of day it is, if you want to set your watch, money! That's how them white boys play the game! Niggers just getting tired of being the only ones supposed to take the ass whipping is what's up on the bricks, cuz!

COMANCHE: We ain't killing anybody but each other.

ROYAL BOY: So the fuck what? White motherfuckers
been fucking each other over since before Noah built
his motherfucking Ark, and you don't hear them
crying about shit. They say fuck that shit, and get about
to the business of making that bank, and living that
life, and if God got a problem with that then He can
bring that shit up on Judgement Day. Man, even then
they probably gonna cut a deal with the motherfucker
anyways. If you got the paper money, you don't do the
time. You learn that shit in kindergarten, man.

COMANCHE: Sounds like the Bed to me.

ROYAL BOY: Man, fuck you! Get the fuck outta my face
with that weak-ass shit!

COMANCHE: Come on, Billy...

ROYAL BOY: Stop calling me Billy, motherfucker, you
ain't got the right! Man, you better stop thinking about
hope and all that voodoo nine soul bullshit, and find a
way to make your way in the world!

COMANCHE: Like you have found your way in the
world?

ROYAL BOY: I have found my own way, because I ain't
had a motherfucking choice! I have made my own
purpose in life! I have picked up those cards that some
sorry-ass God has dealt me, and I am working those
motherfuckers for everything that they are worth!
What about you, bitch? *(Silence)* Man...you ain't
nothing but a crying old woman. What do you got to
give to me?

COMANCHE: I'm gonna check on what's keeping your
public defender.

ROYAL BOY: Yeah, you do that. Find me somebody
that's gonna speak in my behalf. But you find me a
man. You hear me? Find me a real man what got some

motherfucking heart. Find me somebody that ain't you. You hear me, bitch?

(COMANCHE *walks over and picks up the phone and dials. After a couple of seconds he hangs the phone up.*)

COMANCHE: It's busy.

ROYAL BOY: Yeah. Right.

(BABE RUTH *enters the Community Affairs room.*)

BABE RUTH: You seen Cross?

COMANCHE: I thought he was with you.

BABE RUTH: The Captain back?

COMANCHE: No.

BABE RUTH: How's he making out?

COMANCHE: People are getting something together for the family.

BABE RUTH: We been doing that a lot lately around here.

COMANCHE: Things are getting crazy.

BABE RUTH: More than you bargained for?

COMANCHE: No. I'm cool. It's just a lot worse than I remembered, and I remembered it being pretty bad.

BABE RUTH: So you haven't seen Superboy?

COMANCHE: I thought he was with you. You okay?

BABE RUTH: I'm fine. I could just use some sleep.

(BOWIE *enters with some coffee.*)

BOWIE: Hey y'all, I got some of this coffee. Y'all want some?

BABE RUTH: I don't want a thing from you.

BOWIE: A simple no would have been sufficient.

BABE RUTH: Cross is on report. You put him there?

BOWIE: Is that a request, or an order?

BABE RUTH: You make it whatever you want, you just give me an answer.

BOWIE: He was out of control.

BABE RUTH: So were a lot of people. I would reconsider if I was you.

BOWIE: Why?

BABE RUTH: Look, I got my own thing with Cross, and there isn't an ounce of love lost between us, but we handle it in here. Between us. I got an idea about why you are here, and if I'm right, I'm gonna cut you off at the legs and drive a stake through your heart. That is, if I can find one. *(She exits.)*

ROYAL BOY: I'll have some of that coffee. I take mine black.

BOWIE: Fresh out, punk. I thought you took it with cream anyways, you know what I mean?

ROYAL BOY: Fuck you, man.

COMANCHE: You wrote up Superboy?

BOWIE: I have a job to do.

COMANCHE: There was no reason to put him on report.

BOWIE: That's not how I saw it. I have a trust to uphold.

COMANCHE: Trust? What do you know about trust?

BOWIE: I am not going into this with you.

COMANCHE: No, you were talking about trust. The trust you have to uphold. I'd like you to explain to me your idea of trust.

BOWIE: We talking about Cross, or are we talking about you?

COMANCHE: Whichever one you are man enough to discuss with me.

BOWIE: You stepped over the line.

COMANCHE: I trusted you.

BOWIE: I had no choice in the matter.

COMANCHE: You had a choice and you made it.

BOWIE: Well isn't that like the pot calling the kettle black.

COMANCHE: This isn't about back then.

BOWIE: Oh, we only supposed to deal with the part of the past that you want to deal with, is that it? Just like always, right? It's always what you want to deal with, what you want to discuss, the only decision about things that matters is the ones you make for everybody else.

COMANCHE: I guess we both have been holding back shit for a while now, so why don't we come home free and get clean?

BOWIE: Come on with it.

COMANCHE: Look, man, what happened to us? We were brothers, man! We grew up together. Fought our first fights back-to-back. Hell, man, we even got laid together. There was always me and you.

BOWIE: There was also always a third person there, man. You keep forgetting that.

COMANCHE: I ain't never forgot about Cochise. I have lived my life with his memory branded into my soul, brother. But then again for that matter there was also the Big Bad Bed as well, but I ain't talking about them, I'm talking about you and me.

BOWIE: That's the fucking problem!

COMANCHE: What's the fucking problem?!

BOWIE: You forgot about Cochise before his dead body hit the playground!

COMANCHE: That's a motherfucking lie!

BOWIE: You let the Bed walk away from it like Cochise's life never mattered. Like he wasn't never born! Just another dead nigger with no next of kin!

COMANCHE: Who in the hell do you think buried him? I don't remember you helping out with the particulars of that situation!

BOWIE: It was bullshit! You didn't feel anything about him but guilt!

COMANCHE: I felt something!

BOWIE: AND YOU DID NOTHING! ABSOLUTELY NOTHING! You let that sick motherfucker get away with murdering the only motherfucker who showed us there was a more honorable way to run the streets. The Big Bed broke the rules! He hurt one of us! He broke the rules then just like he's breaking the rules now, and you ain't never gonna stand up to him, ever! In fact you bound me to your cowardly word so that my hands were tied, stopping me from doing the right thing, too. And you want to get up in my face, and have the audacity to tell me that you felt something for that brother? WHAT? WHAT COULD YOU POSSIBLY HAVE FELT FOR COCHISE, ME, OR ANYBODY, EXCEPT FOR SAVING YOUR OWN SORRY BLACK ASS?!!

COMANCHE: Man, I loved...

BOWIE: YOU ARE A LIAR!!! YOU AIN'T NEVER LOVED COCHISE IF THAT'S THE WAY YOU LET HIM GO OUT!!!

COMANCHE: I LOVED YOU MOTHERFUCKER!!! IT WAS YOU I WAS PROTECTING!!!

BOWIE: WHO IN THE HELL ASKED YOU TO?

COMANCHE: COCHISE WAS DEAD, MAN!!!
UNDERSTAND? THE BROTHER WAS DEAD!!!
THREE BULLETS IN HIS HEAD DEAD, AND
BROTHER, YOU DON'T GET MUCH DEADER
THAN THAT!!! COCHISE WASN'T GONNA NEVER
SEE THE LIGHT OF DAY OR THE DARK OF NIGHT
EVER AGAIN!!! YOU HAD A PISTOL IN YOUR EAR,
AND THAT LUNATIC MOTHERFUCKER WAS
GONNA BURN YOU RIGHT THEN AND THERE!!! IF
I HADN'T STRUCK THE DEAL...

BOWIE: WHO ASKED YOU TO SPEAK FOR MY
MANHOOD!!!

COMANCHE: MAN, FUCK YOUR MANHOOD!!! I WAS
TRYING TO SAVE YOUR LIFE!!! *(Pause)* The Big Bed
wasn't worried about you. Conscious or unconscious.
He was worried about me! He was worried what I
might do, no matter how many guns he had on me.
The Big Bed was always afraid of me, at least back
then. It was never about you. He knew that I would do
anything to keep harm from coming to you, man.

BOWIE: And why would he know that?

COMANCHE: Because you were my motherfucking
heart, brother. I loved you more than I loved myself.
I would have let the Bed cut me open and rip out
my soul if it would have saved your life. And when
I poured myself out to you, when I felt the demons
crawling up from the deepest part of me, and threaten
to blow me apart as my sanity was cracking into...
you turned me over, man. Like I wasn't nothing to
you. I told you what went down for real inside of that
building and you gave me up!

BOWIE: I had a job to do. You broke the rules.

COMANCHE: Man, motherfuck a rule! The only family
each of us ever knew was each other. Before Cochise,
before the Big Bad Bed, all we had was each other. You

turned me over and didn't even ask for thirty pieces of silver. You say to hell with me? I say to hell with you! You are an infected scab on the wound of humanity, and I don't want to be infected with whatever it is that has gotten you so diseased. You think I hurt your honor? Honor is just another snakeskin to you, Bowie. Love and understanding need to be honored, too.

BOWIE: Look, Comanche...

ROYAL BOY: I don't think he wants any of your coffee, man.

BOWIE: Shut up, punk. I ain't gonna tell you but one time. You think you turned out better than me? Is that it?

COMANCHE: At least I know who looks back at me when I look at the man in the mirror.

BOWIE: Do you?

COMANCHE: Oh, yeah. I know we gotta take this boy down, and he is going down hard.

BOWIE: That ain't our problem.

COMANCHE: Then whose problem is it?

BOWIE: You gotta know the rules to the game or else you can't play. His own fault if he doesn't know that.

COMANCHE: He don't belong in the game, Bowie. He ain't even old enough to make the team. He ain't fumbled the ball, we never handed it to him.

ROYAL BOY: Man, fuck all this, I don't need neither one of you motherfuckers.

COMANCHE: You need us more than you can ever know. I just don't know if I got anything left to give to you. I'm all used up. I probably was more of a help to that Red Skull than I have been to you. But I ain't gonna stop trying. A nigger like me gotta do that if there is any kind of redemption to life. A way of making things right. I'm drowning in the same quicksand that you find yourself in right now. Been in it longer than you. Maybe if you can stand on top of my shoulders, it'll buy you an extra couple minutes of daylight. 'Cause if I don't, you'll disappear before your reflection in the mirror can call out your name. You'll be gone from this world before God gets the news. I have looked into the heart of the abyss and stared straight through myself. But you see, the only difference between Bowie and me is that I know how low I have sunk in the mire. What about you, Bowie?

BOWIE: You wouldn't understand.

COMANCHE: I understand I'm trying to make it back to the surface so I can get a breath of fresh air. What about you?

BOWIE: YOU WOULDN'T FUCKING UNDERSTAND!!!

COMANCHE: THEN MAKE ME UNDERSTAND!!! MAKE ME FUCKING UNDERSTAND!!! WHAT IS WRONG WITH YOU?!! WHAT HAPPENED TO YOU, BROTHER?!!

(CROSS *and* BABE RUTH *come arguing into the Community Affairs room.*)

CROSS: Come on, Babe Ruth, give me a break, alright?

BABE RUTH: You don't deserve a break. This ain't McDonald's.

ROYAL BOY: Whassup, y'all!!!

BABE RUTH: Captain here?

COMANCHE: No. What's going on?

BABE RUTH: Captain's gonna have my ass.

CROSS: He should.

BABE RUTH: Man, you better shut up. I don't want to hear anything coming out of you.

COMANCHE: Something go down?

BABE RUTH: We were working the sheriff angle...

CROSS: Saw some bullshit go down...

BABE RUTH: We got them tipped up on...

COMANCHE: And...

CROSS: She starts yelling at the top of her lungs for the Boys to drop their weapons.

COMANCHE: Yeah?

CROSS: Before we got the drop on them! Fucking child care!

BABE RUTH: You were slow.

CROSS: I WASN'T SLOW!!! I WAS THERE!!!

BABE RUTH: YOU WEREN'T THERE!!! YOU WERE SLOW IN BRINGING YOUR GUN AROUND!!!

CROSS: I'M NEVER SLOW!!!

BABE RUTH: YOU WEREN'T THERE!!! YOUR MIND WAS ON SOMETHING ELSE!!! *(Silence)* You know what I'm talking about too.

COMANCHE: I don't know what you two are talking about.

CROSS: You say something to me?

BABE RUTH: I ain't saying something. I'm saying exactly what I said.

ROYAL BOY: Girlfriend taking your shit out of the toilet and putting it to the curb.

CROSS: SHUT UP BEFORE SOMEBODY SERIOUSLY HURTS YOU!!! I ain't harboring nothing because I ain't regretting a thing.

BABE RUTH: Then why don't you tell Comanche what happened on the porch when Cuba and the Orangutans, you, me, and Miller were all gathered there? That brother wasn't reaching for his weapon...

CROSS: Yes he...

BABE RUTH: HE WAS REACHING FOR HIS KID, MAN!!! HIS LITTLE GIRL!!! YOU OVERREACTED AND SHOT AND KILLED A CHILD, MAN!!!

(Silence)

COMANCHE: This true, Cross?

CROSS: He was reaching for his gun, I swear he was reaching for his gun.

BABE RUTH: You blew her away either way. Bullets started to fly, and Miller was killed as well. And you want to know something funny, Comanche? When they dug out all the bullets, all they got out of Miller was police fucking issue.

CROSS: I ain't hit Miller. I know I ain't hit Miller.

BABE RUTH: Yeah, well, I guess we will never know about that. Maybe you, maybe me, maybe both of us. Only God and his guardian angel know for sure. But you shot the kid. All of that rests squarely on your shoulders. And you can swagger and bullshit your braggadocio shit from now until doomsday, but you came in there like an asshole into a situation Miller and me had under control, overreacted, and shot a child to death. That much is certain. That much now everybody knows.

COMANCHE: This have something to do with the Captain's son getting hit?

BABE RUTH: The child was the Big Bad Bed's niece. He went berserk after that. He declared war and hit the Captain's son, and we have Cross the Superboy to thank for it. You saying I ain't never watched your back? I been covering your ass ever since, and I am tired of covering up your sorry shit. Wipe your own ass from now on.

CROSS: Nothing would have happened if you and Miller weren't on that porch in the first place.

BABE RUTH: Man, how can you try to act like it don't mean anything? What is wrong with you? Doesn't anything bother you at all?

CROSS: Nothing.

BABE RUTH: She was just a little girl, man.

CROSS: No. Nothing bothers me at all. The nigger had no business dealing out of his house. His own damn fault. Understand?

BABE RUTH: Man, I give up.

ROYAL BOY: Yeah, well, the Big Bad Bed ain't gonna give up until he makes your motherfucking ass give up the ghost, motherfucker!

CROSS: Fuck him! He can rub it on his chest!

ROYAL BOY: YOU TRICK HOOK PUNK FAGGOT MOTHERFUCKER!!! YOU SHOOT LITTLE GIRLS AND SHIT, THEN YOU WANT TO PERPETRATE YOU SOME KIND OF MAN AND SHIT!!! I BET THE COUNTERFEIT MOTHERFUCKER PROBABLY GOT A HARD ON WHEN HE TOOK HER OUT BEHIND THAT SHIT TOO!!!

(CROSS *lunges at the cage, with the intent of killing* ROYAL BOY. COMANCHE *and* BOWIE *pull him off.*)

ROYAL BOY: HELP!!! HELP ME!!! POLICE BRUTALITY!!! SEXUAL HARASSMENT!!! CHILD ABUSE!!! WHERE'S THAT HILLARY CLINTON BITCH WHEN YOU NEED HER!!!

COMANCHE: GET IT TOGETHER, CROSS!!! CHILL OUT, MAN!!!

CROSS: I'M GONNA KILL THAT LITTLE MOTHERFUCKER!!!

COMANCHE: IT AIN'T HIS FAULT!!!

CROSS: I'M GONNA KILL HIM!!!

COMANCHE: IT AIN'T HIS FAULT WHAT HAPPENED UP ON THE PORCH!!! IT'S YOURS!!! LEARN TO LIVE WITH IT, MAN!!!

(CROSS *calms down.*)

COMANCHE: Hard as it gets, and it ain't ever gonna get easy, you are gonna have to learn to live with it. Because there is nothing else about it you can do.

(CROSS *goes over to his desk, and sits down. Everything goes quiet for a moment.* FELLOWS *enters the Community Affairs room.*)

FELLOWS: Well… it's nice and quiet in here.

BABE RUTH: What do you want?

FELLOWS: Where's Jabali?

BABE RUTH: He's at the hospital.

FELLOWS: His son?

BABE RUTH: Yes.

FELLOWS: Dead?

BABE RUTH: Yeah.

FELLOWS: Tell him I'm sorry when he comes back, and that I need to see him.

BABE RUTH: I'm sure he'll be touched by your concern.

FELLOWS: I need to talk to you for a minute. Alone.

BABE RUTH: I don't want to do thing one with you alone. You got something to say, say it.

FELLOWS: Just put it out there?

BABE RUTH: I ain't never hid nothing about my life. You got something to say to me, say it.

FELLOWS: Is that the problem?

BABE RUTH: I don't have a problem with you. Now I know who you are.

FELLOWS: And who am I?

BABE RUTH: Somebody who won't let anything get in the way in her rise to the top, no matter how low you have got to go to get there.

FELLOWS: I am no more ambitious than you. You sat around for hours on end complaining about how you were always getting overlooked for promotion.

BABE RUTH: That's not the same thing that I'm talking about!

FELLOWS: Oh, merit had something to do with your situation, but not mine?

BABE RUTH: I ain't gotten anything that I haven't deserved.

FELLOWS: And I have?

BABE RUTH: I HAVEN'T GOTTEN A THING BECAUSE OF WHO I SLEEP WITH, AND WHO I DON'T SLEEP WITH ANYMORE!!!

FELLOWS: NEITHER HAVE I!!!

BABE RUTH: REALLY?

FELLOWS: REALLY!!! I AM NOT SLEEPING WITH THE GOVERNOR!!!

BABE RUTH: YOU COULD HAVE FOOLED ME!!!

FELLOWS: I AM SICK OF THIS SHIT!!! DAMMIT, RUTH, I WOULD HAVE EXPECTED THIS KIND OF BULLSHIT FROM THEM, NOT FROM YOU!!! I

THOUGHT YOU KNEW ME BETTER THAN THAT!!!
I THOUGHT YOU AT ONE TIME CARED ABOUT
ME!!!

BABE RUTH: I DID CARE ABOUT YOU!!! DAMMIT, I
STILL DO!!!

(Silence)

FELLOWS: I see…I thought…

BABE RUTH: You ain't thought about nothing but
yourself. You and your career. That's all you ever
talked about. That's all that ever mattered.

FELLOWS: That's not true. You know that's not true.

BABE RUTH: Do I?

(Pause)

FELLOWS: Maybe you don't. Maybe you're right, and
I'm wrong. But the truth of the matter is I am not
sleeping with anybody, if the truth has to be known
in this room all out in the open this way. You need to
publicly embarrass me so that you can feel better, okay.
You got it. But think about this for a second, okay?
Maybe the fact is that I didn't break up with you so I
could move up the political ladder at all. Maybe the
reason I broke up with you had only to do with you.

(Silence)

BABE RUTH: I haven't a thing to say to you that isn't
going to be in my report.

FELLOWS: That will be sufficient enough when you
complete it. Thank you. Sorry to interrupt you,
Commander Milano. *(She exits.)*

ROYAL BOY: I guess you ain't getting you none tonight.

BABE RUTH: Superboy…tape and cuff that sonuvabitch.

CROSS: Affirmative.

BABE RUTH: Anybody have a problem with that?

COMANCHE: No.

BOWIE: Do what you want.

BABE RUTH: I ain't got two words to say to you, Bowie. Just stay out of my face.

BOWIE: That's six words.

BABE RUTH: You think I'm playing? I look like somebody's toy?

BOWIE: What did I do to you? I haven't done a thing to you.

BABE RUTH: I have had just about my fill of all you unconscious motherfuckers surrounding me in this room. Just stay clear of me for the rest of my life. You do your jobs, and I'll do mine. I'm gonna request a transfer out of here because I am so sick and tired of putting up with all of y'all's bullshit!

COMANCHE: What am I supposed to have done?

CROSS: She the confused motherfucker dragging her heart behind some chick, finally decided that her way of loving just don't measure up. Sounds like a personal problem to me, baby.

(Pause)

COMANCHE: All of us don't feel that way, Babe.

BABE RUTH: You lie, Comanche.

COMANCHE: Cross just misses A J, we all do. It's been a kind of tough day on all of us.

BABE RUTH: You keep wanting to play that A J card, and every time you put it down Comanche, it's to cover some bullshit that is going down in here. The truth is nobody here is as messed up about his suicide as they are by the fact that nobody knows why he did it. They worried about whether they the next to crack, not about poor A J so I don't want to hear you mention

it to me anymore. See, A J was the only one of you
who was a straight up human being. With him gone
all I got surrounding me here is you, and I am sick of
y'all. I gotta put up with stupid remarks, and stupid
attitudes, I have to wade through so much shit to do
my job I should be floating. You see, fellas, I am who I
am because of what I want life to kick back to me. Not
because I'm a freak, not because I have some incurable
disease, but because I can love, which I know is an
alien emotion to you.

CROSS: I ain't gonna try to be nice…

BABE RUTH: Why don't you try being a man, brother.

CROSS: What?

BABE RUTH: A man. Ever hear of it?

CROSS: What the fuck you talking about?

BABE RUTH: I'm not talking some fake kick-ass hope-
to-be-mistaken-for-a-real-man, you know what I'm
saying?

COMANCHE: Why do you think we are wearing these
badges? What do you think that's about?

BABE RUTH: I don't know, Comanche. I don't have a
clue about what that's about. But I can tell you what it's
not. It's not about respect. You all talk your bitch this,
your motherfucker that, you all ain't nothing really but
a bunch of gangsters when it all comes down to it, and
that's exactly what you have wanted to be your whole
entire life. I mean, what can these boys possibly learn
from you? Maybe what they can learn from you is the
exact same thing they learn from the Big Bad Beds of
the world. You ever think about that? The thought ever
cross your mind? Have you ever showed them how
to take responsibility for the shit that they do to other
human beings, or have you showed them through your
bellyaching about the white man that they don't have

any power over their own lives anyways? What do
you know about the Royal Boy? What do you know
about him, Comanche, since you came back to the
Untouchables all enlightened and shit? You know he
saw his father gunned down in the streets right before
his eyes? The Big Bad Bed did. He found the punk who
killed him, and blew his brains out. Nobody else did a
thing about it. Nobody else cared. Then the Bed took
that boy's mamma. Got her on the pipe, and turned her
all the way out. Nobody did a thing about that either.
He fucked and kicked her ass whenever he wanted,
dogged her in public, and threw her away when he
was through with her. All done right in front of that
boy. See, the Big Bad Bed is showing all of these boys a
way. A way without decency, sympathy, or morality.
Take whatever you want, you don't have to respect
nothing, not even your own mother. You see I am used
to you motherfuckers falling short. There wasn't a man
around me on the day I was born, and frankly I don't
see one standing around me now. I got work to finish.
Because y'all haven't done your job with these boys as
men, I gotta do mine as a cop. I gotta put another piece
of our future away. Why don't you all try putting your
little minds together, and come up with something that
will keep it from getting to that in the first place. You
know what I'm saying?

(BABE RUTH *grabs some things off of her desk and goes into*
JABALI'*s office.*)

(*Silence*)

COMANCHE: I'm gonna see what's taking the kid's
lawyer so long. (*He exits the Community Affairs room.*)

CROSS: Say, man, did you put me on report?

BOWIE: I pulled it.

CROSS: You pulled it? I thought...

BOWIE: A lot of people are thinking a lot of things today. I pulled it. All right?

CROSS: Okay. Thanks.

BOWIE: Skip it. I'm going to go get some coffee from downstairs. You want some?

CROSS: Yeah.

BOWIE: Black, sugar, or cream?

CROSS: Does it matter?

BOWIE: It always matters, Superboy. Sometimes more than we know.

(BABE RUTH *comes out of* JABALI's *office.*)

BABE RUTH: I'll take some coffee too. Especially if I am going to stay awake long enough to finish these reports.

(BOWIE *nods and then exits.*)

CROSS: Babe Ruth?

BABE RUTH: What do you want?

CROSS: It does.

BABE RUTH: Does what?

CROSS: Bother me.

BABE RUTH: Yeah?

CROSS: That girl wasn't any older than my own sister, you know what I'm saying?

BABE RUTH: I know.

(*An* ASSASSIN, *played by* THE SIGNIFYING MONKEY, *enters the scene in a long black coat.*)

CROSS: I didn't want to die.

ASSASSIN: You can't always get what you want.

CROSS: What?

ASSASSIN: But if you try sometimes you get what you need.

BABE RUTH: Who the hell are you?

ASSASSIN: The Angel of Death, motherfucker!

(The ASSASSIN *rips open the coat and pulls out an automatic weapon and begins firing.* BABE RUTH *pushes* CROSS *out of the way, but before she can get off a round she is hit. The* ASSASSIN *wheels on* ROYAL BOY *and is ready to shoot him, but* BOWIE *comes back in gun blazing and takes out the* ASSASSIN. CROSS *holds* BABE RUTH *in his arms.)*

CROSS: Oh my God…

(End of Scene One)

Scene Two

THE SIGNIFYING MONKEY:
If you ever find yourself lost in the jungle
surrounded by wild cannibal enemy beasts
with hungry motherfucking teeth
then you know your ass is in trouble
cuz it took a bunch of a hundred years to
put your ass there
and it gonna take more confusion
than blackness
to catch a ride on out
before the nigger in you explodes
all bleeding and weeping
up inside of a memory you done forgot
leaving nothing avenged

ROYAL BOY: So what the fuck, man?

COMANCHE: You gotta talk to me, Billy.

ROYAL BOY: You ain't got no more permission to use my name.

COMANCHE: Look, Billy, it's gonna get real rough around here, you hear what I'm saying?

ROYAL BOY: You can't harm a newborn baby versed in the supreme mathematics, brother.

COMANCHE: The Big Bad Bed baptizing babies for the Five Percent Solution these days?

ROYAL BOY: I know what's righteous!

COMANCHE: What you're doing, want to join, is righteous? Robbing, doping, roping, and smoking is what the knowledgeable say is righteous?

ROYAL BOY: What makes what magic you got working for you more important, more righteous than what I gotta use, man? What you know about me?

COMANCHE: What?

ROYAL BOY: What you know about me, man? You don't know nothing about nothing. You don't know that voodoo shit you be faking any better than I understand what the Big Bed be saying.

COMANCHE: I'll give you that.

ROYAL BOY: No, you don't believe in your voodoo, man. Even when it works for you ya just can't believe in it. But I believe in the Big Bad Bed. He enlightens me, homey. What do you got you can touch with your hand? Your badge? Uniform? Shit…if you believed in your gun you would at least make some kind of sense.

COMANCHE: What kind of sense?

ROYAL BOY: Shit, the best kind. You'd have some motherfucking respect! A nigger with a PhD ain't nothing but a nigger, homes. But a nigger with a PhD and an AK-47 motherfuckers call sir, man. These white boys don't call nobody "sir" they don't fear.

COMANCHE: Who said that?

ROYAL BOY: Caligula and Hitler, motherfucker. Two bad assed white-boys.

COMANCHE: Now that sounds like the Big Bad Bed talking.

ROYAL BOY: They scared a lot of motherfuckers, man!

COMANCHE: Compared to what? Why are you so eager for a one way ticket to the graveyard?

ROYAL BOY: Shit, man, ain't that where I'm headed anyways? I reiterate, motherfucker, what do you know about me? Anything? *(Silence)* You see, I am sick and tired of all you niggers looking down on me. Telling me what I need to be whole without knowing a goddamn thing about me. All you social working motherfuckers, you teachers, cops...

COMANCHE: That how I come off to you?

ROYAL BOY: What have you got to give me that some white man ain't given to you.

COMANCHE: The knowledge of who you are!

ROYAL BOY: Fuck, there's that knowledge word again, man. You sure he ain't gave you that, too, man? I mean looking at you I ain't too sure.

COMANCHE: If I don't own nothing else, I own that. I know that.

ROYAL BOY: A motherfucking history lesson? Who gives a fuck, man. My present is all fucked up. What do you know about that? You think your history lesson is gonna feed my ass and my baby's, man?

COMANCHE: Your what?

ROYAL BOY: The past ain't the past in the hood, man. It's the present, man. Everyday! I don't want it to be my future, homey.

COMANCHE: You got a baby?

ROYAL BOY: Yeah, I got a kid, so what?

COMANCHE: You're nothing but a child.

ROYAL BOY: Shut up motherfucker.

COMANCHE: You nothing but a child!

ROYAL BOY: Fuck you!

COMANCHE: You don't need to be anybody's daddy, goddammit!!!

ROYAL BOY: So, I'm a daddy!!! Can't you get next to that, motherfucker?!!

COMANCHE: You need a father, not a baby, Billy!!!

ROYAL BOY: STOP CALLING ME BILLY, MAN, YOU AIN'T GOT THE RIGHT!!! Fuck you, man! You think you and me the same nigger? You think you know me? What do you know about me, man? What do you know about me? About me? ME!!!!

COMANCHE: Nothin'.

ROYAL BOY: What?

COMANCHE: Nothin'.

ROYAL BOY: What?

COMANCHE & LADY IN WHITE: NOTHIN'!!!

LADY IN WHITE: NOTHING!!! NOTHING!!! I DON'T KNOW ANYTHING ABOUT YOU!!! NOT A GOD DAMNED THING!!! ALL I KNOW IS THAT YOU ARE A FUCKING LITTLE PUNK!!!

ROYAL BOY: WHAT?

LADY IN WHITE: YOU ARE FUCKING NASTY FILTH AND I HOPE YOU DROWN IN THE SHIT YOU HAVE SURROUNDED YOURSELF IN YOUR WHOLE FUCKING LIFE!!! FUCK YOU, YOU LITTLE MOTHERFUCKER!!! YOU LITTLE BLACK MOTHERFUCKER!!!

ROYAL BOY: WHAT DID YOU CALL ME, BITCH!!!

LADY IN WHITE: YOU BLACK MOTHERFUCKER!!!
YOU BLACK MOTHERFUCKING NIGGER!!!

(ROYAL BOY *puts the gun right between her eyes, on her forehead.*)

ROYAL BOY: COME ON, YOU MOTHERFUCKING
BITCH!!! TALK SOME OF THAT NIGGER SHIT
NOW, MOTHERFUCKER!!!

LADY IN WHITE: FUCK YOU!!! PULL THE TRIGGER!!!
I DON'T GIVE A SHIT!!! I HAVE DRAWN MY OWN
GODDAMN LINE RIGHT HERE!!! YOU'RE NOT
TERRORIZING ME ANY GODDAMNED MORE!!!
YOU WILL HAVE TO KILL ME IF YOU WANT TO
LAY A HAND ON ME!!! YOU HAVE THE GUN!!!
FUCK YOU, USE IT!!! I DRAW THE LINE RIGHT
HERE!!!

(Silence)

ROYAL BOY: Shit, baby. You ready to fight me to the
death, ain't you? Don't care whether you die or not,
just ready to go to war to the bitter motherfucking
end. You just sick of my ass and you ain't gonna
take it anymore. Man, that is just how I feel. In a
motherfucking nutshell.

LADY IN WHITE: I haven't done anything to you. I don't
even know you.

ROYAL BOY: How can life get so fucked up? Shit just
gets all ugly and twisted, life is just shitty, you know?

LADY IN WHITE: I don't want to do this. Talk to you.
Get to know you…

ROYAL BOY: Can't hold on to nothing. Can't belong to
nothing.

LADY IN WHITE: I don't want to know you, know
anything about you…

ROYAL BOY: We don't know shit about nothing about each other, ourselves, nothing. You know what I mean?

LADY IN WHITE: No.

ROYAL BOY: I saw my baby boy being born. I mean, that shit was great. The motherfucking best, you know? My girl wasn't no chickenshit behind it neither. She being nothing but thirteen.

LADY IN WHITE: Oh God.

ROYAL BOY: Naw, man. She was hard like a motherfucker. I mean, we ain't shit but kids, our bodies might be a little ahead of schedule, but what the fuck do we know you know? We just hoping and praying and wishing and dreaming, trying to prepare ourselves to deal with a miracle. Me going, "push it, baby, push it, push, push, push, yeah, call me every kind of dirty motherfucker you want for getting you into this shit, but keep breathing and keep on pushing little mamma. Kick my ass, but keep on pushing." She throwing down like she heavyweight champion of the world and shit, all scared and hurting, looking all lost and shit, but battling with a heart bigger than the ocean. Fighting with everything she got, and then BOOM!!!... there the little motherfucker is, you know what I'm saying? I look at him, I look inside of his eyes and I see me, man. I see my soul in his eyes. I tell him, "You the man. You ain't gotta worry about shit, I got your back for motherfucking life." It was the first time I felt proud of being me. Felt good about being alive. Man, that shit was magical, you know what I'm saying? Now ain't no motherfucking magic left. Now there ain't nothing left but some fucked up chickenshit bullshit.

LADY IN WHITE: Things might be different for your baby. It has you, doesn't it? You gotta believe in that, you gotta have hope.

ROYAL BOY: MOTHERFUCK A HOPE!!!
MOTHERFUCK ALL THE HOPE THERE IS IN THE
WORLD!!! HOW COULD YOU SAY THAT TO ME?!!
LOOK WHERE OUR ASSES ARE RIGHT NOW!!!
LOOK AT THE FUCKING BULLSHIT WE ARE
UP TO OUR EYEBALLS IN!!! WHAT HOPE YOU
GOT DROWNING IN THIS SHIT WITH ME, HUH
SNOWGIRL?!! YOU, MY JUNKIE ASS MAMMA,
MY STUPID FUCKING GIRLFRIEND, ALL YOU
MOTHERFUCKING BITCHES GETTING YOUR
ASSES KICKED ALL OVER WEST HELL AND SHIT,
Y'ALL AIN'T DONE SHIT TO NOBODY, BUT LIFE
KICKS YOUR TEETH IN ANYWAYS, AND YOU
GOT THE NERVE TO WANNA TALK ABOUT SOME
MOTHERFUCKING HOPE!!!

LADY IN WHITE: You don't want to do this.

ROYAL BOY: SHUT UP!!! SHUT THE FUCK UP!!! IT
DON'T MATTER WHAT I WANT, IT JUST MATTERS
WHAT I GOTS TO DO, YOU KNOW WHAT I'M
SAYING?!!

LADY IN WHITE: You don't wanna kill me, you're
nothing but a baby...

ROYAL BOY: I'M GONNA KILL YOU, BITCH!!! I'M A
COLD-BLOODED MOTHERFUCKER, DON'T GIVE
A SHIT ABOUT NOTHING BUT KILLING AND
DYING!!! YOU DON'T KNOW NOTHING ABOUT
ME!!! YOU DON'T KNOW NOTHING ABOUT ME!!!

LADY IN WHITE: Oh, God, I can't take this anymore.
Your fucking problems, it's not my fault, I don't even
know you, IT'S NOT MY FAULT!!! DO YOU HEAR
ME?!! IT IS NOT MY FUCKING FAULT!!!

ROYAL BOY:
SHUUUUUUTTTTTTTTUUUUUUUUPPPPPP!!!!!!!!!!!

(The lights go out suddenly. We hear a gunshot in the dark. Lights return to normal.)

COMANCHE: I ain't got no home for you, Billy. I ain't got enough to build it.

ROYAL BOY: You just gonna walk out on me, man. How you gonna do that, homey?

COMANCHE: I can't do it. I gotta go! Own yourself, man!

ROYAL BOY: I can't own myself! Nobody ever stuck around long enough to show me how! I GOTTA BELONG TO YOU!!! YOU CAN'T RUN OUT ON ME NOW!! DO YOU HEAR ME?!! WHO GONNA OWN UP TO ME, WHO AM I GONNA BELONG TO?!!

(BOWIE enters.)

BOWIE: What in the hell is going on in here?

ROYAL BOY: I GOTTA BELONG TO SOMEBODY, MAN!!!

BOWIE: How about your new roommate in the hole, kid?

COMANCHE: Bowie...what?

BOWIE: Come on, kid. Time to check out your new rent. Captain thinks you gonna like it.

COMANCHE: What are you talking about Bowie?

ROYAL BOY: Fuck you!

BOWIE: Does the name Doghouse Maniac ring a bell?

COMANCHE: Bowie! You can't put him in the hole with that sick motherfucker!

BOWIE: Captain's orders. Come on.

ROYAL BOY: Nooo...

COMANCHE: What is wrong with you, man?

BOWIE: For the last time, Comanche, not a goddamn thing. I do what I do, I've done what I've done, because I am who I am. You gotta be who you gonna be a hundred percent of the time, or you are nobody… nothing.

COMANCHE: Who were you when you turned me over, man?

BOWIE: Motherfucker, I turned you over to get you out, brother! This shit on the bricks is too thick for you, Comanche. You might have caught a shotgun blast in the stomach, but you ain't never had the gut for the Cut. It always was. If you had wasted the Big Bad Bed a long time ago, you might have saved a lot of lives. You might have lost me mine, but you might have saved Estelene Raye's life for her. Maybe that's why you flipped out on that Red Skull, brother. You ever think about that? You a walking time bomb full of guilt and regret, and you gonna explode all over yourself someday. My advice, after careful observation, is best get off the tracks before the train wreck comes. You just a nigger trying to come back from losing your mind. Let the dead bury the dead. It ain't a job for heroes. Run. Please.

(BOWIE *and* ROYAL BOY *exit.*)

THE SIGNIFYING MONKEY: Now you are a part of the truth.

COMANCHE: But I don't understand anything. I don't know anything!

THE SIGNIFYING MONKEY: You are a part of the truth. You are a part of the truth like a branch is part of the tree. You must seek out the other branches to understand the whole. But remember this warning… the thirst of the dead must be relieved.

(A strobe light comes on. COMANCHE, CROSS, JABALI,
BOWIE, *and* FELLOWS *enter in character. They move in a
style that says entrapment, anger, and fear. The lights fade
up slowly as they are all in place, and* JABALI *and* FELLOWS
exit his office.)

FELLOWS: Look, Jabali, all hell is about to break loose,
and come down on us like a ton of bricks.

JABALI: On us?

FELLOWS: Yes, on us. We are going to have T V news
teams coming out of the cracks in the walls in a minute
over something like this! A gangland hit in a police
station?

JABALI: I know what it was. It was my station house!

FELLOWS: We are going to get a reputation for this kind
of thing soon if we don't watch out.

JABALI: There is no "we" involved in this situation,
counselor. I don't believe "we" are going to take a fall
when heads come to being chopped off.

FELLOWS: Oh, yes we are. The Governor has promised
me whatever fate befalls you, befalls me. You go down,
I go down. So, like it or not, I am a part of this unit
until further notice…

JABALI: I don't like it! I'm getting a little tired of you,
the Governor, and all of your little political games!
Either you tell the Governor to give me the number of
people I have requested from him when I first saw all
of this coming, or you can handle the situation and the
press by yourselves! You can have my badge and find
somebody else to deal with the gangs!

*(*FELLOWS *starts to exit the Community Affairs room, then
stops and comes back over to* JABALI.*)*

FELLOWS: Ruth still in critical condition?

JABALI: Yes.

FELLOWS: They say yet what her chances are of…have they said whether or not her condition is improving?

JABALI: Still touch and go. But the Babe Ruth is tough. She's a fighter.

CROSS: She's the toughest cop in the Untouchables. Her heart ain't gonna let nothing take her nowhere she don't wanna go.

FELLOWS: I know that. Believe me I know that. *(She starts to fight off tears.)*

JABALI: You all right, Fellows?

FELLOWS: I'm fine. Look… Alright, you got it. Whatever you need. If I can't get it for you, I'll kick somebody's ass until I get it. I want the Big Bad Bed hanging from a meat hook in deep freeze somewhere at the bottom of the world. I'll do whatever I can do to help.

JABALI: Keep in touch.

(FELLOWS exits the Community Affairs room.)

CROSS: You think Babe Ruth is gonna be okay?

JABALI: They say it's too early to tell, but that it doesn't look good. She got hurt real bad. *(Silence)* Okay, get over it. We have work to do. Listen up! The jungle is on fire. It's worse than a thousand Devil's Nights out there tonight. We gotta get to the Big Bad Bed, and wipe him off the face of the earth before he turns the city into *Apocalypse Now!*

COMANCHE: You want me to bring up the kid?

JABALI: No, I want Bowie to do it. He hates Bowie. Don't worry, with the Doghouse Maniac sharing the hole with him, he should be glad to see you. You did good taking out the Bed's assassin, Bowie.

BOWIE: Thank you, Captain.

JABALI: Go and get the kid.

BOWIE: Yes sir. *(He exits.)*

JABALI: Superboy!

CROSS: Yes, Captain?

JABALI: I want you to go to Dunning Playground, and casually check out these explosions that have been happening up there all evening. No reason for me to believe it isn't the Big Bad Bed. But step like a feather. It smells like a trap. You have a bad shot so you have to avoid physical contact if at all possible. If you get a clear shot at the Big Bad Bed, take him out. We will deal with the consequences later.

CROSS: Captain, I'm a little…

JABALI: You gotta get back on your horse sometime, Superboy. I need to keep both Comanche and Bowie here, my best bet in getting the demon is crack the kid through extreme interrogation. You just gonna have to pull your own weight. Understand?

CROSS: Yes, Captain. I never meant to intimate that I couldn't, sir.

JABALI: You just stay on task, be frosty, and wide awake. Remember what I said about the Bed. You have a clean shot, take him out. Be ever vigilant and be ready.

CROSS: Born that way, Captain. *(He exits.)*

COMANCHE: Captain…

JABALI: I don't want to hear it, Comanche.

COMANCHE: You know Superboy hasn't any kind of business out there on the bricks solo, Captain. You are using him to bait the Bed, aren't you, Captain?

JABALI: Didn't you hear what I said, Sergeant? I'm through with it.

COMANCHE: You just gave an order which amounts to putting out a contract on the Big Bad Bed, and you have the Royal Boy locked in the hole with the Doghouse Maniac!

JABALI: So?

COMANCHE: You read the report on the Royal Boy's time in juvie reform. You know the Doghouse Maniac sexually assaulted...

JABALI: The report said "physically accosted"...

COMANCHE: You know how to read between the lines on a report...

JABALI: No complaint was filed...

COMANCHE: DAMMIT CAPTAIN!

JABALI: WATCH YOUR TONE AND LANGUAGE WITH ME, SERGEANT CUMMINGS!

COMANCHE: What you are doing to that kid is inhuman and disgusting!

JABALI: I refuse to let this boy become the future line of our precious blood, Comanche! I do not care about the cost!

COMANCHE: But, Captain, if we give up on him, what kind of future are we going to have? If we don't try to, who else is going to save him?

JABALI: He cannot be saved, Comanche! We cannot climb Jacob's Ladder with trash like the Royal Boy dragging us back down every time we reach another rung on the ladder. There are laws! There can be no margin for error!

COMANCHE: But didn't I break those same laws when I beat that Red Skull to death?

JABALI: You didn't break them, you enforced them!

COMANCHE: By murdering another human being?

JABALI: You murdered no one! You can't murder a cold blooded killer!

COMANCHE: Then what did I do? What would you call it?

JABALI: You became the righteous arm of the avenging angel of God!

COMANCHE: How can you know, how can you be so sure, Captain? I'm not.

JABALI: I know because I have walked the night with the avenging angel of darkness before!!! I have called down Oshagun, the Militant Christ, felt the full fire of his fury, and made Him do my bidding!!!

COMANCHE: What are you talking about, Captain?

JABALI: You sit up here, reading your book, looking for some kind of forgiveness that will set your guilt free, trying to find a God, any God, that will give you absolution for your sins. Well, Comanche, God helps those who help themselves. The answer isn't forgiveness, it's retribution. I have lived it. When I was a boy I saw my father lynched, right before my eyes in our front yard. The Ku Klux Klan murdered him because he wouldn't be anything less than a free man of dignity. They held me down and forced me to watch it. My neighbors, my colored neighbors, who laughed and joked with my father underneath that same tree he hung from...stood by and did nothing. NOTHING!!! Those niggers just shook their heads, prayed to their blond haired, blue eyed Jesus, and went back to their miserable lives. I swore to myself, then and there, I would never be like them. I paid them Klan boys back. Every single last one of them. A J and I visited them in their sleep one night, and slit their throats from ear to ear. He held them, and I cut them. You see, Comanche, some things cannot be forgiven. Only avenged. You keep looking for what you don't need.

COMANCHE: You don't know what I need, Captain, and what does any of this have to do with the Royal Boy anyways? He's not a member of the KKK, but a true manchild lost in the promised land. Your kind of retribution for his isn't justice, it's genocidal suicide!!!

JABALI: THERE IS NO JUSTICE!!! MY FATHER, MY SON, ESTELENE RAYE, THAT POOR WOMAN, EVEN A J DIDN'T GET ANY JUSTICE!!! BUT THERE CAN BE SOME ORDER!!! AND THERE WILL BE LAW!!!

COMANCHE: WHAT LAW?!!

JABALI: AN EYE FOR AN EYE, COMANCHE!!! AN EYE FOR AN EYE!!!

COMANCHE: WHAT ABOUT. "VENGEANCE IS MINE"?!! WHAT ABOUT THAT LAW?!!

JABALI: VENGEANCE!!! WILL!!! BE!!! MINE!!! *(Silence)* Now, I'm through with this conversation, Comanche. You are either going to work on my side, my way, or you can take your voodoo hoodoo and your black behind out of here right now. Do you understand me?

COMANCHE: What's the difference then between them and us, Captain. What's the difference?

JABALI: AM I UNDERSTOOD, SERGEANT?!! YES OR NO?!!

(Pause)

COMANCHE: Yes sir.

(BOWIE *brings in* ROYAL BOY.)

COMANCHE: "And let the games begin", said Caesar as they brought the lion to the Christians.

ROYAL BOY: Hey, man, I'm gonna tell my lawyer about this shit, motherfucker!

JABALI: You want me to send for her now?

ROYAL BOY: I don't want that bitch y'all gave me, man! Come on! You gonna give me a bitch to defend my ass for rape? I didn't come down with yesterday's rain, man!

COMANCHE: Don't you think a woman would be better for you in this case…?

ROYAL BOY: FUCK YOU, MAN!!! That bitch hated me!

BOWIE: Oh, I can't imagine that.

ROYAL BOY: Fuck you!

JABALI: You made noises downstairs about having something to say.

ROYAL BOY: I ain't saying shit until I get another lawyer!

JABALI: Fine with me. Take him back to the hole!

ROYAL BOY: WAIT MAN! YOU CAN'T PUT ME BACK DOWN THERE!

JABALI: Why not?

BOWIE: Something wrong with the accommodations?

ROYAL BOY: You know what the fuck is wrong, man!

JABALI: No, I don't. What's wrong, your Royal Badness?

ROYAL BOY: You got that big assed snaggle toothed motherfucker down there trying to…you know what I'm talking about?

BOWIE: A little crowded down there in the hole?

ROYAL BOY: Y'all is messing with me, man! Put me somewhere else!

JABALI: No vacancies. You got something to tell me?

ROYAL BOY: Fuck you!

JABALI: Not what I was looking for. Take him back.

ROYAL BOY: NOOOO!!!!

JABALI: Look, you got something to talk about, fine. If not, you can go back to your little bridal suite and wait to see another lawyer. Might take some time, though. Might take hours. You catch my drift? Can you understand English when it's being spoken to you? I'm waiting, and your roommate is getting awfully lonely. What's it gonna be?

ROYAL BOY: Y'all ain't right, man.

JABALI: The whole world is wrong, Royal Boy. Been that way for as long as anybody can remember. And mercy is in short supply. I'm tired of trying to be fair with you. Life isn't anyways. You gonna either have to talk, fight, or…get the picture?

BOWIE: Your Royal Badness.

JABALI: Your choice, little brother. *(Silence)* Well?

ROYAL BOY: What do you want to know?

JABALI: What do you think?

ROYAL BOY: I don't know, man. You tell me. Whatever you want, okay?

JABALI: Okay. Who had the gun?

(Pause)

ROYAL BOY: There weren't no gun.

JABALI: There was a gun involved.

BOWIE: She was shot to death.

JABALI: Remember?

BOWIE: Remember how she was shot?

JABALI: Shot from the gun of a rapist?

ROYAL BOY: No, how was she shot?

BOWIE: She took one to the womb, buddy. The bullet hit her where the good Lord split her.

JABALI: Remember?

ROYAL BOY: What kind of gun are you talking about, man?

BOWIE: How about the one that killed her.

JABALI: That is not in question. There was a gun.

BOWIE: The Captain just wants to know which hand you put it in.

JABALI: Which hand did you have the gun in, your Royal Badness?

ROYAL BOY: There wasn't a gun!

JABALI: Oh, there was a gun. A gun killed the woman. How come we know there was a gun there, and you don't?

BOWIE: Your Royal Badness.

JABALI: That has me downright puzzled.

COMANCHE: Maybe it wasn't your gun?

JABALI: There's a thought.

BOWIE: You know we got you stone cold on the rape.

ROYAL BOY: Wasn't nobody raped!

JABALI: Rape, aggravated assault, kidnapping, violation of her civil rights…

ROYAL BOY: How I violate a white girl's civil rights?

BOWIE: By killing her, punk!

JABALI: It doesn't look good.

BOWIE: Your Royal Badness.

JABALI: How many rounds you fire?

COMANCHE: Maybe the gun was fired by somebody else?

BOWIE: Now there's a thought.

JABALI: A better thought.

BOWIE: How many shots you say you fired?

ROYAL BOY: I didn't fire any shots. The gun belonged to...

JABALI: Who did the gun belong to, Royal Boy?

ROYAL BOY: It didn't belong to nobody.

BOWIE: You trying to tell me that gun just stood up and shot and killed that poor woman all by itself?

JABALI: Better get your lies together.

BOWIE: You sounding confused. Weak. Limp-wristed.

ROYAL BOY: Fuck you!

BOWIE: No, I think it's gonna be fuck you up the ass big time for the rest of your life, you know what I'm saying?

ROYAL BOY: Ain't you gonna fine him some money for, like, swearing and shit?

JABALI: I'M GETTING TIRED OF PLAYING AROUND WITH YOU, BOY!!! I ALREADY GOT YOU KNOCKED ON THE RAPE AND POSSESSION!!! YOU TALK TO ME NOW, RIGHT NOW, AND TELL ME WHAT I WANT TO KNOW OR YOU CAN GO BACK TO THE HOLD AND GET A GREAT BIG GIANT MONSTER DOSE OF YOUR OWN MEDICINE!!! I WANT IT, AND I WANT IT NOW!!!

ROYAL BOY: I...I...I...

COMANCHE: Who was on it with you, Billy? Who was leading the Wild Bunch attack?

BOWIE: You said "we" earlier?

JABALI: "We seen her!"

COMANCHE: Who was "we"?

ROYAL BOY: I DON'T KNOW!!! What could I get for manslaughter?

BOWIE: Manslaughter? Don't make me laugh!

ROYAL BOY: Motherfucker, don't laugh at me!

JABALI: You are down for murder one!

BOWIE: The Big Boy. That's the gas chamber, chump.

ROYAL BOY: You can't do that to me! I'm a fucking minor!

BOWIE: Oh, ain't you heard? There's a new law in the land, punk. Proposition Thirteen. They just passed it last night. It says for heinous crimes like what you copping to, there ain't no age limits no more. The gas chamber is an equal opportunity employer now.

ROYAL BOY: YOU'RE LYING!!!

JABALI: No, he's not.

BOWIE: You could read it in the paper, that is if you could read.

ROYAL BOY: YOU'RE LYING!!! YOU'RE A LYING MOTHERFUCKER!!!

COMANCHE: No he's not, Billy. He's speaking the truth!

BOWIE: They gonna take that sweet little rump of yours and send it to the Red Wing, and hold you there until you own stock in the mother, then transfer that nice firm butt of yours to death row when the time is all nice and ripe. All those old-time, for-real original gangsters gonna know just how to warm that tasty behind up for the electric chair, baby. You know what I'm saying?

JABALI: You mean gas chamber.

BOWIE: Sorry, I forgot. That takes a much longer time.

COMANCHE: It was the Big Bad Bed that did it all, wasn't it, Billy?

BOWIE: You ain't gonna take this butt screwing for him, are you? I know the nigger. He don't care thing one about you. Come on, you can't be that stupid?

COMANCHE: He'd turn you over in one minute to save himself. You know that's true.

JABALI: What's it gonna be? You gonna be smart or stupid? Choose!

BOWIE: Maybe he ain't gotta choice but to be stupid. He obviously ain't the sharpest tool in the shed!

ROYAL BOY: MAN, YOU BETTER QUIT ALL THAT LAUGHING AT ME!!! I'M FOR REAL MOTHERFUCKER!!! I'LL BE ON YOUR ASS LIKE ON THE ABOMINABLE SNOWMAN, MOTHERFUCKER!!!

(JABALI, *in a move as swift as quicksilver, snatches* ROYAL BOY *and pitches him across the room, startling everybody with the suddenness of the violence.*)

JABALI: COME ON, PUNK!!! SHOW ME HOW BAD YOU ARE!!! I'LL SNATCH YOUR HEART RIGHT OUT OF YOUR BODY!!!

ROYAL BOY: HEY, MAN!!!

COMANCHE: What the hell are you doing, Captain?

BOWIE: What are you doing?

JABALI: SHUT UP THE BOTH OF YOU!!! YOU HEAR ME?!! NOT ANOTHER WORD OUT OF EITHER OF YOU!!! (*To* ROYAL BOY) You gonna be a man? You wanna be a man? The Police Boys gonna make you a man? Just like the Big Bad Bed? Let's see you be a man! Get up and be a man with me!!!

(JABALI *picks him up and throws him again.*)

ROYAL BOY: DAMN, MAN!!!

JABALI: YOU A LYING, NO GOOD, STANKY LITTLE
YELLOW PUNK!!! YOU AIN'T WORTH WHAT
FALLS FROM THE CRACK OF MY BEHIND!!!

ROYAL BOY: MAN, QUIT SWEATING ME, MAN!!!
GET AWAY FROM ME!!!

JABALI: The Big Bad Bed is your pimp!!! He's pimping
your manhood all up and down the streets like you
ain't nothing but a one dollar ho!!! He's turned you out
like a high school virgin!!!

ROYAL BOY: FUCK YOU!!!

(JABALI *snatches* ROYAL BOY *and whips him into the air
and against a wall.*)

ROYAL BOY: OOOOOOOOOOWWWWWWWWWW!!!

JABALI: I have had to put up with punks like you my
entire blessed life! Ain't no difference between none of
y'all. The Police Boys, or them Klan boys who hung my
father in front of me. They wouldn't leave it alone, so
I couldn't leave it alone. The Police Boys can't leave it
alone.

(JABALI *slams the kid against the wall again.*)

JABALI: STOP CRYING, PUNK!!! LISTEN UP, HARD
GUY!!! YOU ARE GOING TO THE JOINT!!! YOU
FOLLOW ME?!! WHAT LITTLE MANHOOD YOU
THINK YOU HAVE, THEY ARE GOING TO PUMP
YOU UNTIL YOU FORGET WHAT IN THE HELL SEX
YOU ARE!!! YOU THINK I'M SWEATING YOU? BOY,
YOU HAVEN'T EVEN BEGUN TO COMPREHEND
WHAT BEING SWEATED TRULY MEANS!!!

ROYAL BOY: Man, you're crazy!!!

JABALI: Oh, you are so right, punk! In the last two days
I have lost two people who were more dear to me than
my own life!!! You got enough size in your pants to
back off somebody who has truly lost their mind?

(JABALI *snatches* ROYAL BOY *again.*)

ROYAL BOY: GET OFF ME, MAN!!!

JABALI: GET ME OFF YOU, PUNK!!! COME ON, GO
FOR BROKE!!! LET'S SEE HOW MANY LEVELS YOU
GOT, YOUR ROYAL BADNESS!!! YOU CAN'T EVEN
KEEP ME FROM TAKING YOUR SWEET LITTLE
BEHIND RIGHT NOW IF I HAD A MIND TO!!! CAN
YOU?

(JABALI *pushes* ROYAL BOY *to his knees.*)

COMANCHE: JABALI!!!

JABALI: SHUT UP!!! I COULD DO ANYTHING TO
YOU THAT I WANTED TO RIGHT NOW!!! YOU
AIN'T GOTTA WAIT TO GET TO THE JOINT TO BE
TAKEN DOWN!!! I COULD DO IT RIGHT NOW!!!
COMANCHE, BOWIE, LEAVE THE ROOM FOR A
MINUTE!!! TIME TO GIVE THIS PUNK HIS LAST
LESSON!!! HIS WARM UP BEFORE THE BIG SHOW!!!

COMANCHE: DAMMIT, CAPTAIN!!! BILLY, PLEASE
TELL HIM WHAT HE WANTS TO KNOW NOW!!!
WHO RAPED AND KILLED THAT POOR WOMAN!!!

ROYAL BOY: I FUCKED THE BITCH I KILLED THE
BITCH I FUCKED THE BITCH I KILLED THE BITCH
WHAT DO YOU WANT ME TO SAY WHAT DO YOU
WANT ME TO DO FUCK ALL OF YOU MAN HOW
MUCH SHIT DO YOU WANT TO TAKE FROM ME
HOW FUCKING MUCH?!!

COMANCHE: WHO WANTS SOMETHING FROM
YOU, BILLY?!! WHO IS RIPPING YOU FROM
YOURSELF?!!

ROYAL BOY: YOU ARE RIPPING ME FROM MYSELF!!!
ALL OF YOU!!!

COMANCHE: THE CAPTAIN!!!

ROYAL BOY: YEAH!!!

COMANCHE: ME!!!

ROYAL BOY: YEAH!!!

JABALI: THE BIG BED!!!

ROYAL BOY: RIGHT!!!

COMANCHE: HE TOOK OFF YOUR MOMMA, RIGHT?!! BILLY?!! AM I RIGHT?!!

ROYAL BOY: FUCK MY MOTHER!!! THAT JUNKIE DON'T GIVE SHIT ONE ABOUT…

COMANCHE: THEN WHAT DID HE TAKE FROM YOU, BILLY?!! YOU GOTTA TELL ME!!! I'LL HELP YOU PAY THAT SONUVABITCH BACK!!!

ROYAL BOY: ESTELENE, MAN!!! SHE WAS MY GIRL, MAN!!! SHE WAS THE MOTHER OF MY…GODDAMMIT, MAN!!! GOD DAMN IT!!! Goddammitgoddammitgoddammit!

COMANCHE: (Sweet, blessed, Jesus.)

ROYAL BOY: He made me choose between Estelene and my baby, or him. I couldn't choose them. What the fuck could I have done for them? I chose the Bed, he laughed in Estelene's face, and she called him a bastard and slapped the shit out of him. He came down on her hard.

BOWIE: (That sonuvabitch.)

ROYAL BOY: Can't nothing belong to me? Can't I belong to nobody? Does everybody have to keep taking everything away?

COMANCHE: Don't you get it, Billy? We don't want you. We just want to get the Big Bad Bed. Give him up and we can let you walk through those doors right now. Come on, Billy. You don't owe him a damn thing. Save yourself. What do you say?

ROYAL BOY: It's funny, man.

COMANCHE: What is?

ROYAL BOY: You guys not wanting me…shit… Y'all just a bunch of motherfuckers added to a long line.

COMANCHE: Billy, you have to give the Captain an answer, man.

JABALI: What's it going to be, your Royal Badness?

(Silence)

ROYAL BOY: Go and get Snowgirl, man.

JABALI: Bowie, go get Fellows now.

BOWIE: I'm on it, Captain.

COMANCHE: What are you going to tell Fellows, Billy?

ROYAL BOY: Whatever y'all motherfuckers want.

JABALI: Just as long as I can burn the Big Bad Bed into eternity and longer. Everybody gonna get some payback today.

ROYAL BOY: Y'all don't care about me one way or another.

JABALI: What do you think?

COMANCHE: I care, Billy.

ROYAL BOY: Shit…you can't even care for yourself, Scarface. How you gonna care about me?

JABALI: Just tell Fellows about the Big Bad Bed, and you ain't gotta worry about anybody ever worrying about you again.

(BOWIE *enters with* FELLOWS.)

FELLOWS: You got something for me?

JABALI: A Special Bulletin for Eyewitness News.

FELLOWS: Will it hold up?

COMANCHE: It'll hold up.

FELLOWS: Okay, Comanche, in lieu of a stenographer, you take his statement for the record. All right, give it to me straight. Why don't you tell me what everybody else already knows.

ROYAL BOY: I did it. All by myself. I fucked her, and I shot her.

FELLOWS: What in hell is going on here, Jabali?

JABALI: I don't know!

COMANCHE: BILLY!!!

ROYAL BOY: I told you once, man, you ain't got the right to call out my name anymore as long as you live. You had your chance to represent me. All of you did. Fuck all of y'all!!! I did her, man. All the way. I did it because I was bored, and had nothing better to do.

COMANCHE: Man, don't do this. Don't do this to me...

ROYAL BOY: To you... Fuck you, bitch! I just wanted some action, something to happen. I wanted to be a Police Boy, to belong. You gotta belong somewhere... right? That's where I belong.

JABALI: That it?

ROYAL BOY: Ain't no other truth you getting from me.

JABALI: All right, have it your way.

(The phone rings in JABALI's office. JABALI answers the phone.)

JABALI: Ninety-ninth Precinct, Captain LaRouche speaking...yes, that sounds wonder...what...when... I'll be right down.

FELLOWS: What happened? It's Ruth, isn't it?

JABALI: Babe Ruth's condition has been upgraded from critical to serious. She's not out of the woods, but she has regained consciousness.

FELLOWS: Thank God. I'll go down to the hospital with you.

JABALI: I'm not going to the hospital. I'm going to Dunning to identify Cross.

COMANCHE: What?

FELLOWS: Oh my God.

JABALI: He was killed. It was an ambush. The Police Boys.

ROYAL BOY: I told you suckers not to fuck with the Big Bad Bed!

JABALI: I HAVE HAD ENOUGH OF YOUR MOUTH, ROYAL BOY!!!

COMANCHE: Shit, Captain! Goddammit, man!

JABALI: Comanche! Stay on task!

ROYAL BOY: FUCK YOU PUNKS!!!

JABALI: BOWIE!!! TAKE THIS PUNK BACK TO THE HOLE!!! NOW!!!

BOWIE: BUT THE DOGHOUSE MANIAC IS STILL DOWN THERE!!!

JABALI: DO LIKE I SAY!!!

ROYAL BOY: NAAAAWWW, MAN!!! YOU CAN'T SEND ME BACK DOWN THERE, MAN!!! I AIN'T GOING BACK DOWN THERE!!!

FELLOWS: NO, CAPTAIN, YOU CAN'T PUT HIM DOWN THERE!!!

(BOWIE grabs ROYAL BOY who starts struggling with him viciously.)

COMANCHE: I SHOULD HAVE KILLED THAT NIGGER!!! I SHOULD HAVE KILLED THE BIG BAD BED WHEN I HAD THE CHANCE!!! MOTHERFUCKER!!!

ROYAL BOY: YOU TOO PUSSY A MOTHERFUCKER
TO FUCK WITH THE BIG BAD BED!!! FUCK YOU,
FUCK THAT BITCH SUPERBOY MOTHERFUCKER,
FUCK THAT BULLDAGGER, FUCK ALL OF Y'ALL!!!

COMANCHE: SOMEBODY SHUT HIM UP!!! SHUT HIM
THE FUCK UP BEFORE I KILL HIM!!! YOU HEAR ME
YOU MOTHERFUCKING PUNK?!!

JABALI: COMANCHE!!!

ROYAL BOY: COME ON, BITCH!!! I'M DOWN WITH
IT!!!

(ROYAL BOY *spits in* COMANCHE's *face.* COMANCHE
explodes with a great sudden rage. He snatches ROYAL BOY
away from BOWIE, *and begins to choke him, trying to tear
his throat apart with his bare hands.* BOWIE, JABALI, *and*
FELLOWS *all try to pull* COMANCHE *off, but he is a frenzied
Hercules and subdues them all violently with the rage of a
hundred thousand madmen.)*

BOWIE: COMANCHE!!!

JABALI: COMANCHE, STOP!!!

(JABALI, *who has recovered enough to see that* COMANCHE
is about to snap ROYAL BOY's *neck, pulls out his pistol and
shoots* COMANCHE. COMANCHE *falls on* ROYAL BOY, *who
is crying and gasping for air. A silence, then…)*

BOWIE: SOMEBODY CALL A FUCKING
AMBULANCE!!!

COMANCHE: ESU, DON'T UNDO ME!!!

THE SIGNIFYING MONKEY: I am the scorn of all my
adversaries…

COMANCHE: I have become a broken vessel…

THE SIGNIFYING MONKEY: O I hear the whispering of
many…

COMANCHE: Terror on every side…

THE SIGNIFYING MONKEY: As they scheme together against me...

COMANCHE: As they plot to take my life. I gotta get clean...

JABALI: Gotta get it out...

COMANCHE: But God helps those...

JABALI: Who help themselves. *(He takes his badge off.)* God helps those who help themselves.
I been wading in the bloody waters my whole life...
Since before the rock of ages I been smothered in the devil's blood...
I have had the smell of his demon sweat blowing my nose wide open...
Since before the day I was born. I will study the ways of the ugly one no more! I throw you out of my body... Out of my mind! Out of my heart...
Through my very soul!
O Impious demon!
I cast you out!
You who have been tossed down from the heavens and thrown into the pits of hell!
I cast you out!
I exorcise you Devil! In vain shall you boast about this deed!
When Almighty God takes back a sinner, you no longer have any rule over their spirit!
I expel you out from all your strongholds!
I expel you out from the marrow of our souls!
I CAST YOU OUT!!!
AND CUT OFF YOUR ARMS!!!
DELIVER YOUR SPOILS TO THE FIRE FROM
   WHICH THEY CAME!!!
RETURN ALL WHO FOOLISHLY BOUND
   THEMSELVES TO YOU!!!

YOUR POWER HAS COME TO NOTHING!!!
I FOREVER BREAK MY BLOOD PACT WITH YOU
THAT WHICH WAS WASHED IN THE BLOOD OF
   THE GOAT!!!
I RETURN MYSELF TO THE ALMIGHTY ONE!!!
THE ONE WHO MADE JESUS WALK THE WATER,
AND MOVED THE MOUNTAINS TO
   MOHAMMED!!!
IN THE NAME OF THE FATHER AND THE SON,
I CHOOSE NOT TO DIE!!!
IN THE NAME OF THE FATHER AND THE SON,
I CHOOSE NOT TO DIE!!!
IN THE NAME OF THE FATHER AND THE SON,
I CHOOSE NOT TO DIE!!!
BUT!!! TO!!! LIVE!!!
I AM FOREVER WASHED IN THE BLOOD OF THE
   LAMB AND THE HOLY ONE!!!
FOR THINE IS THE KINGDOM, AND THE POWER,
AND THE GLORY!!!
THINE IS THE KINGDOM, AND THE POWER, AND
   THE GLORY!!!
BECAUSE THINE IS THE KINGDOM, AND THE
   POWER, AND THE GLORY!!!
WORLD WITHOUT END—FOREVER AND EVER
   AND EVER AND EVERMORE!!!
AMEN!!!

(ROYAL BOY *begins to cry, weeping as a little child lost in the world.* JABALI *hears it, and he reaches out to him, and cradles him in his arms and rocks him like you would rock a baby.*)

JABALI: Have mercy...sweet Lord...have mercy.

THE SIGNIFYING MONKEY: Now you belong to me.

COMANCHE: Bowie...

BOWIE: I'm sorry, man. What is it, brother?

COMANCHE: I can feel it. Washing up against the darkness.

BOWIE: What can you feel, Comanche, what can you feel, man?

COMANCHE: The circle of knowledge. For the first time, man...I didn't know who I was until today.

BOWIE: Who are you, homes?

COMANCHE: I am the prince of the royal blood...I am the Silver Surfer.

(BOWIE *cradles* COMANCHE *as he dies in his arms, as* JABALI *cradles* ROYAL BOY, *as Sweet Honey sings* Jacob's Ladder. *As* THE SIGNIFYING MONKEY *smiles the lights away.)*

END OF PLAY